LIVING TO WIN

THE FIVE ENDURING PRINCIPLES OF SUCCESS

Bo Short

EXCALIBUR
PRESS

First published in the United States of America in 2000 by Excalibur Press, Inc.

Cover design by Anne Matthews, Image Creations Graphic Design.

Library of Congress Catalog Card Number: 99-75787

ISBN   0-9658207-1-8

How to Order:
Living To Win may be purchased for
educational, business, or promotional use.
For information contact Executive Books at
(800) 233-2665, or fax at (717) 766-6565.
Visit our website: www.executivebooks.com

To my wife, Sandy, and our little girl, Taylor.
You are my life. I thank God for you everyday.

Contents

INTRODUCTION

This book was not designed to just make you feel good about your potential. Nor was its purpose to simply tell you that you can make your dreams come true. Besides those things, I wanted to challenge you, to dare you to step out from the crowd and embrace your future... to do something great with your life. You risk too much if you do not. We live in a time when we are all too accepting of the premise that:

It doesn't matter whether you win or lose, it's how you play the game.

I, for one, could not disagree more. Please understand that playing with integrity is critical. In fact, if you have to cheat to declare victory then you have not won at all. Playing with character is paramount to lasting success. However, I contend that it **does** matter if you win or lose. I believe that your life depends on it.

Excelling in all areas of your life, including family, health, spiritual, and financial brings abundant rewards. Failing can be devastating.

Statistics tell us that:

- By 1990, **parents were, on average, available 10 hours per week less to their children** than they were in 1980 and 40% less than in 1965.
- 75% of all married couples would have 1 parent stay home full-time with the children **"if money were not an issue."**
- Almost 45% of **juvenile violent crimes** occur between 3pm and dinnertime.
- 92% of **children on welfare** today are from **broken families**.
- Divorced and separated people experience acute conditions such as infectious and parasitic diseases, respiratory illnesses, digestive disorders, and severe injuries **significantly more frequently** than other marital status groups.
- The combined effects of marriage and worship on **income levels** in a national sample of young adults tracked for 20 years by the US Department of Labor is stunning. There is a **50% difference in the lowest and highest groups**—between those who grew up in a broken, non-worshipping family and those who grew up in an intact, regularly worshipping family.

Source: *The Breakdown of the Family- The Consequences for Children and American Society*...Patrick F. Fagan

In the news you hear about children's soccer leagues that have instituted a "no scoring" policy. High schools that have decided to recognize numerous valedictorians, as well as multiple homecoming kings and queens. In this move to protect peoples "feelings," we are lowering the performance bar and finding "less" to be acceptable.

While turning our attention to pass/fail exams we are overlooking a very important fact. That is simply this: **life keeps score**. It rewards those who win.

Living to Win is a battle cry to encourage you to step into the fight, overcome your obstacles and make your dreams come true. Through my own success, I have seen first hand that anything is possible. Years of studying great success stories in sports, business, politics, and the arts, have convinced me that there are certain key principles that one must adopt in order to gain victory.

I discuss each one of them within the covers of this book. Read it, and **go do something great with your life!**

CHAPTER ONE
VISION

"A rock pile ceases to be a rock pile the moment a single man contemplates it, bearing within him the image of a cathedral."
– Saint-Exupery, Flight to Arras (1942)

Having a vision is imperative to success. Vision is an essential ingredient in living to win. In fact, you can trace the importance of having a vision all the way back to the Bible. Proverbs, chapter 29, reads, "Where there is no vision, the people perish." It has also been said that even a child building a sand castle has some kind of picture in his or her head telling them what to do next. It's vision. If you want to become a leader in business, government, entertainment or athletics — if you want to be successful in any significant endeavor — you first need to have vision.

In order to understand the power of vision let me demonstrate how, throughout history, great people succeeded because they dared to dream, sometimes despite huge obstacles. I also want to encourage you to develop your own ambitious vision for what you want to accomplish in your life. Understand that there are no constraints on the human mind... no walls around the human spirit... and absolutely no barriers to our vision except those we build ourselves.

Every enterprise, whether it's beginning a business, starting a family, running for elected office, teaching a class, or serving as a leader in the military, to name just a few, is based upon a vision. The significance of vision goes to the core of leadership. Vision is inseparable from leadership. Vision links the present to the future through the person of the leader.

The philosopher and educator Alfred North Whitehead said, "Great dreamer's dreams are never fulfilled, but they are always transcended."

Frederick Faust once said, "There is a giant asleep within every man and when the giant awakes, miracles happen." I agree with this because I have seen so-called miracles happen in my own life.

I grew up in the shadows of the Washington Monument and the Lincoln Memorial just across the Potomac River from our Nation's Capital. It was there that I first began to understand the power of a dream and the belief that it could come true. I saw my father, who was born in the small town of Moultrie, Georgia, be the first in his family to attend college, rise to become the Chief of Staff for the longest serving United States Senator in history. My father lived his dreams. He has worked on Capitol Hill for more than two decades and he is annually named one of the 50 most powerful staff members in Washington. He has dined with presidents, kings, heads-of-state, and people from all walks of life. Both of my parents instilled in me the belief in the power of dreams, as long as we were willing to dream big and work hard enough.

I have witnessed supposedly ordinary men and women accomplish extraordinary feats. Why? Why were they able to accomplish what had previously been considered impossible or, perhaps, had never even been contemplated at all? It's simple— they had vision.

I want to encourage you to study the lives of people who have achieved great things. If you want to be an entrepreneur, you should study great entrepreneurs... if you want to be successful in business, study the lives of great businesspeople... if you want to be a great composer or an attorney, then study the lives of great composers and great attorneys. Don't study failure. Study success —only then will you understand how to emulate it and achieve it yourself.

It was Sir Isaac Newton, the father of science, who said, "I have seen so far because I have stood on the shoulders of giants." Newton was describing how his vision was extended by studying the vision and the work of the great scientists who came before him. It worked for Newton and it is vitally important in our own lives.

Oftentimes when I speak in schools, businesses, and civic groups I am amazed by the number of people who tell me that they were taught, "It's a tough world out there, do the best you can do, but if things don't work out it's ok." What a devastating thing to impart to your children. It raises my spirits when people tell me that they were told, "If it's been done before, you can do it." Well, my parents took it one step further. They said, "Even if it's never been done before, you can do it." What a powerful statement for a child to carry into adulthood. Even if it has not been dreamt of — you can do it. This unleashes unlimited possibilities in a child's mind.

This is one of the most important points about vision. If you can think it, you can do it. Great thinking leads to great results. Conversely, mediocre thinking leads to mediocre results. We can accomplish anything as long as we dare ourselves to reach for it.

The author and well-known business consultant Peter Drucker wrote that the number one difference between Nobel Prize winning scientists and all other scientists was that they asked bigger questions. The Nobel Prize-winning scientists did not have higher IQs. They were smart, but not necessarily smarter than other scientists. They did not work any harder. But the key was they thought bigger… they dreamed bigger… they asked bigger questions. They reached higher with their minds.

For you, a big dream might be a family or a house. A big dream might be to start your own business and own it, or build your existing business bigger than anyone else can imagine. Your dream might be to achieve a major breakthrough and make a significant contribution to society. Whatever it is, ask the big questions. Dream big.

With vision, there are no age restrictions. There are no size requirements. There is no minimum down payment needed. Again, if you think it, then you can do it.

And I guarantee you this: Having a vision for your life, being a visionary, does not guarantee that people will applaud you. Chances are, you may have to struggle to get others to see what is so apparent to you. You will likely run into people who say, "It can't be done, it's impossible." Or they might say, "It may be possible, but you're sure not the person who is going to get it done."

The Power of Vision

Dr. Wayne Dyer, a professor at St. John's University, used to tell his colleagues that he would become a best-selling author. This was long before he ever had anything published. They laughed. Well, to date, Dr. Wayne Dyer has sold more than 58 million books. I wonder if his university colleagues are laughing now.

Let me give you another real-life example of what I'm

talking about. For the better part of 16 years now, Steve Case has nurtured a vision. Back in the days when computer modems creaked along at 300 bits a second... when it took half an hour to download a small black-and-white photo... and when many Americans were obsessing over CB radios, Steve Case imagined a world where ordinary people could do great things with computers that were connected to each other.

Most people considered that to be a perfectly ridiculous idea. In 1985, Steve Case, as you may know, founded a company called America Online — or, AOL. Since then, Case has fought an almost daily battle with people who seriously doubted his vision. In fact, in 1987, his most loyal supporters, his Board of Directors, nearly decided to fire him.

So how is Steve Case's vision looking now? Well, last September he was on the cover of TIME Magazine. Led by Case, AOL has become cyberspace's first true empire. It is a global online service that is adding 6,000 new members a day and will soon be available in more than 100 countries.

And now, the Board of Directors at AOL are saying, "Well, I guess Steve was right." I'm telling you this because I want you to see and understand the power of vision.

Let me ask you some important questions. How big are your dreams? What is your vision for the future? Have you written down your vision? Have you shared your vision with anyone who is important to you? Have you spoken your vision out loud?

You see, I'm a firm believer that you can speak your vision into reality. Consider for a moment the revolutionary impact of John F. Kennedy's bold and unexpected pronouncement that the United States would send a man to the moon within 10 years. His words established a new benchmark... a new standard for what people considered possible in space travel. And as you know, eight years and two months after President Kennedy's bold statement, Neil Armstrong walked on the moon's surface and said, "One small step for man, one giant leap for mankind."

I had the good fortune of having lunch with the production manager for the lunar module program. He said the rallying cry of President Kennedy bonded a group of people with a common vision. People came in early and stayed late. They didn't need to use a time clock. The vice president of the program kept his desk on the production floor and would walk around asking people, "do you know why you're here? Do you know what our goal is? Do you share the same vision?"

That's vision. That's what vision can do. It can put a man on the moon. A vision can extend the horizon of your own life. President Kennedy once said, "The problems of the world cannot possibly be solved by skeptics or cynics whose horizons are limited by the obvious realities. We need men who can dream of things that never were."

So you need to ask yourself, what are my dreams? Where do I want to go?

Let me give you an example of how vision can shape a career in business. Fred Smith was a graduate student at Yale when he wrote a term paper about the overnight delivery of mail. The story goes, by the way, that Smith received only a C+ on the paper. But he had a vision. After graduation, he founded a company called Federal Express.

The initial vision statement for Federal Express was, "We will deliver the package by 10:30 the next morning." Just think how Fred Smith's ambitious vision and his willingness to say it out loud has revolutionized the way we do business in America today, and around the world.

Well, maybe you have a business plan written down somewhere but you can't quite get yourself to take it out of your desk drawer. Here are some facts that might motivate you to live to win... to pursue your dream. Today, Fred Smith's company, the thing he dreamed up in a term paper, has $13.3 billion in revenue... 142,000 employees worldwide... a vehicle fleet of 40,000... an air fleet of 615 planes. That's more than the entire air force of some countries. Fed Ex now covers 90 percent of the world within 24 hours.

There's nothing you can't do if you have a vision... and are dedicated to fulfilling that vision. Create the highest, grandest vision possible for your life because you become what you believe.

Oprah Winfrey said, "When I was a little girl living in Mississippi, growing up on the farm, I remember watching my grandmother through the screen door boil clothes in a big iron pot because we didn't have a washing machine. We had to make everything we had. I watched her and realized that inside myself, in the spirit of myself, that although this was segregated Mississippi and I was 'colored' and female, that my life could be bigger, greater than what I saw around me. I remember being four or five years old, I certainly couldn't articulate it at the time, but it was a feeling inside that I allowed myself to follow. I had a vision for what I could become.

I am proof that anything is possible. I think that my life... the fact that I was born where I was born, at the time that I was, and have been able to do what I have done speaks to the possibility of following a vision. It's not that I'm special, it's that I had a feeling of what I could accomplish. People should hold the biggest possible vision for themselves."

There was a study done among many of the men and

women who survived the Nazi concentration camps during World War II. One of the survivors was a Viennese psychiatrist named Victor Frankl. He was one of the only people who left Auschwitz alive. Except for his sister, Victor Frankl's entire family perished. His parents, his brother, his wife all died in the Nazi camps or were sent to the gas chambers.

Frankl himself suffered torture and countless human indignities. The people conducting the study wanted to know what separated him from the other people who didn't make it out of the concentration camps. Frankl was brought before an auditorium full of people and here is what he said to the audience: "There is only one reason I am here today, what kept me alive was you. Others gave up hope. But I dreamed. I dreamed that someday I would be here telling you how I, Victor Frankl, had survived the Nazi concentration camps. I've never been here before, I've never given this speech before, but in my dreams I have stood before you and said these words a thousand times."

Victor Frankl's vision — in this case, his vision of achieving freedom — was powerful enough to literally keep him alive. Even in the most inhumane conditions, Frankl realized that his Nazi captors could not take away his freedom to dream big dreams.

Vision Motivates Action

Having a vision gives us tremendous purpose in our lives. In Victor Frankl's case, having a vision literally meant the difference between life and death. For us, having a vision means that we are passionate about it, it raises our energy level. We may have hundreds of goals that we want to achieve, and which we do achieve as we go along. Our vision keeps us looking and moving forward.

Survivors of POW camps in Vietnam and elsewhere have reported experiences similar to Victor Frankl's. They say that a compelling, future-oriented vision is the primary force that kept many of them alive. The power of vision is absolutely incredible!

Research shows that children with what is called "future-focused role images" perform far better in school and are significantly more competent in handling the challenges of life. Teams, businesses and other organizations with a strong collective vision outperform those without the strength of vision. According to the Dutch sociologist Fred Polak, a primary factor influencing the success of entire civilizations is the "collective vision" people have of their future.

Vision is the best manifestation of our creative imagination. Vision is also the primary motivation behind human action. The opposite is also true: if we don't have a compelling vision for the future, we are, by definition, not as motivated as we can or should be. Vision is the ability to see beyond our present reality... to imagine what does not yet exist... to become someone new... to achieve at a higher level. Vision gives us the capacity to look forward and live out of our imagination rather than look backward and live out of our memory.

Vision provides an overall context for our lives. Without a vision, we are basically reactive, we react to what other people value and want from us. We fall into the trap of trying to become all things to all people... trying to meet everybody else's expectations... and we end up meeting nobody's expectations, especially our own. But with a clear sense of .

vision, all the advice that we solicit, all the feedback we get, makes sense in the context of our vision. We can process the information in a way that is useful. We can build on it. We can move closer to actually achieving our vision.

Having a vision and achieving it is like the process of repentance and forgiveness. Repentance is not an event. Forgiveness is not a moment. It's a process. We don't say, "I'm sorry" and it's over. It's a process. We repent and then we work toward forgiveness. The same is true of vision. We develop a vision, we shape it and refine it and work toward it. It's a process that moves us forward as we live to win.

We all have some vision of ourselves and our future. That vision opens doors of opportunity and it also creates consequences. Perhaps more than any other factor except our character, vision affects the choices we make and the way we spend our time.

If our vision is limited, we tend to make choices that are based on what is in front of us. If our vision only extends to what's on TV tonight or what we hope to do during the upcoming weekend, then obviously, our vision will not take us very far. If our vision is limited then we tend not to think very far ahead. We react to whatever seems urgent on a specific day or at a particular moment. We get sidetracked by other people's priorities. We vacillate and fluctuate based on the day. We don't go forward, we end up going sideways. It's as though we drift.

If our vision is based on illusion, then we tend to get discouraged when we are confronted with challenges and adversity. If our vision is only partial, if it focuses on just one aspect of our lives, like our jobs, then we tend to get out of balance. If our vision is based on someone's expectations, then sooner or later we will actually get alienated by the vision rather than motivated by it.

Your vision must be built on what you are passionate about achieving in your life. It has to be focused on something you know you want. It could be starting a business… it could be growing the business you are already in… it could be running for office and getting elected… it could be writing a great novel. Your vision can and will lead you to accomplish anything and go anywhere if it clarifies your purpose in life… gives you direction and meaning, and empowers you to perform beyond your resources.

The Olympic motto is the Latin phrase, "Citius, altius, fortius." It means, swifter, higher, stronger. In a sense, this is the vision for the Olympic Games. It is the ideal that guides all of the competition. You will know deep inside your soul that your vision is right for you if it makes you move swifter, reach higher, and become stronger.

Vision can and should become the DNA of our lives. It should become so ingrained and so integrated into every aspect of our being that it becomes the compelling impetus behind every decision we make. It is the fire in our belly. It is the energy within us that makes our life a dynamic, exciting adventure. Our vision can literally enable us to transcend fear, doubt, frustration, discouragement, rejection and many other events or factors that keep us from living our dreams. Vision will help overcome our own perceived weaknesses. It will help us grow and develop our strengths.

I understand that life is full of uncertainties. You may have a vision but you cannot know at this point exactly where you will take your life. Well, that's okay. The important thing, the essential thing, is to have a vision.

Did you happen to see the movie "Forrest Gump?" Even he was concerned about the vision for his life. Forrest asked his mother, "What's my destiny, mama?" She replied, "You're going to have to figure that out for yourself, Forrest." We all have to figure out our own destiny. And the official starting line is vision.

Some people literally visualize what they want to accomplish. This is similar to actually speaking your vision into reality. Whether you are in search of a happy marriage or a tremendously successful career, it's imperative that you can see it in your mind's eye. Act it out in your mind. You must rehearse your success.

Olympic athletes can often be found before an event with their eyes closed scoring a perfect 10 on the balance beam, or being the first to break the tape in the marathon. They're taught that their success will be a result of that which they first see happening in their minds. Great musicians can close their eyes and feel the music before a note is actually played. Military strategists foresee their opponents' movements played out on computer-generated models before making a decision to follow the best, most strategic course of action. There is a lot of medical evidence to indicate that even seriously ill people can improve their health through visualization. Corporate leaders discuss the impact their decisions will have, sometimes years in advance, before actually implementing them.

Walt Disney actually envisioned his movies in his mind before filming them. In fact, he was one of the developers of story boards. Disney also is reputed to have required his staff to meet every morning at 7:30 AM at their Burbank studios and follow a ritual where they would point to their temples and say, "My imagination creates my reality." How right he was. What we dream is what we can achieve.

Jack LaLanne, the health and fitness king, says he

visualized himself going from a lightweight, scrawny youngster to a strong, healthy, robust man who would gain fame and fortune by promoting health to others. He's a walking, talking advertisement for the gospel of good health, and he's been on TV promoting it for more than 40 years.

Muhammad Ali, one of the finest boxers in history, visualized himself as "The Greatest" and actually told the media, "I'm the greatest!" before his first bout with Sonny Liston in which he won the heavyweight championship. As Ali continued his career, he began predicting the round in which he would knock out his opponent. He visualized doing it. And, in many cases, he did it!

John Maxwell, in his book *Developing the Leader Within You,* says that we all live under the same sky but we don't all have the same horizons. This is true. The horizons that we set for ourselves define how far we will go. And history is filled with anecdotes of men and women who clearly lived under the same sky but had vastly different horizons.

From Henry Ford to Walt Disney... from George Washington to Margaret Thatcher... from Steven Jobs and Steve Wozniak to Bill Gates, it would be impossible to imagine their accomplishments without a vision. From the Model T Ford to the hand-held computer, world history has been shaped by innovators — men and women with a vision.

The great success of companies like Wal-Mart, Ben and Jerry's, Microsoft, and Quixtar has been achieved through the inspired vision of one or two people.

Vision Becomes Motivation

The greatest moments in American history are marked by leaders with extraordinary vision. But America's founders were sons and daughters of Europe... the seeds of vision were planted there. Anton Signorile, the noted Italian historian, suggests that vision is a trait born in the immigrants even before they arrived in America. In fact, the type of person who was drawn to America was already a dreamer. Indeed, since Christopher Columbus, the vision of America has fired the imagination of the world. The vision of America has been different things for different people at different times in history.

During the Potato Famine, Irish fathers would describe a bountiful land with rich soil, and a vast ocean to keep away the blight that continually ruined their crops in their homeland. Italian shepherds, crowded by the mountains on one side and the sea on the other, dreamed of acres of abundant grasslands in America's Great Plains, the world's bread basket. Jews in Czarist Russia could describe a land of religious and cultural freedom, where one could openly be a Jew without fear of persecution.

Well, many of the Italians never reached the Great Plains and many of the Irish never found fertile soil of their own. Most of them never got out of the city. And Jews found that bigotry existed in the New World just as they had experienced in the Old World.

But here's the point: It was the dream, the vision of America that motivated them and kept them going. No serious setback or heavy dose of reality ever shook the mythology of

America or the dream and the optimism that the immigrants brought with them. They created an ideal in their minds, a vision, and they tenaciously went about the work to achieve a better life for themselves and their families.

It is still happening today. The boat people of Vietnam...the Cubans who flee the Communist rule of Fidel Castro... the men and women who line up every morning outside of American embassies in the former Soviet Union so they can be granted a visa to come to the United States. What is it that drives them to America's shores? It's the power of their vision.

The very creation of the United States, and the survival of the United States, which today is the freest, the fairest, the most prosperous nation in the history of our planet, was willed by men and women of great vision. Have you ever read the documents that give voice to the vision of America? The Declaration of Independence, Lincoln's Gettysburg Address, Martin Luther King, Jr.'s "I Have A Dream" Speech. It's vision that created this nation, and is still creating it at this very moment.

George Washington, the Father of America, was able to bring the 13 original colonies together because he was able to visualize and articulate an independent, historically unique America. How unlikely it must have seemed that we might become the United States — how uncertain that a Republic could or would be created out of the unexplored wilderness that was America in the early 1700s.

Years later, when America was nearly ripped apart by the Civil War, as brother literally fought against brother, Abraham Lincoln's vision of *the* United States rather than *these* United States kept us together. A century later, Dr. Martin Luther King, Jr. stood on the steps of the Lincoln Memorial and updated President Lincoln's vision with his famous speech.

As I said a moment ago, it has been said that we all live under the same sky but we all have different horizons. What follows is the best story I've ever read that proves this point in the most literal of manners.

In *A Saviour For All Seasons* it reads, "There was a Bishop from the East Coast who many years ago paid a visit to a small, Midwestern religious college. He stayed at the home of the college president who also served as a professor of physics and chemistry. After dinner, the Bishop declared that the millennium couldn't be far off because just about everything about nature had been discovered and all inventions conceived. The young college president politely disagreed and said he felt there would be many more discoveries. But then the Bishop began to challenge the president to name one such invention and the president replied that he was certain that in 50 years, man would be able to fly.

'Nonsense,' sputtered the outraged Bishop, 'only angels are intended to fly.' The Bishop's name was Wright. He had two boys at home who proved to have greater and more ambitious vision for the future than their father. The boys' names were Wilbur and Orville. The father and his sons certainly lived under the same sky, but they had completely different horizons."

It's what you see... It's how big you see things.

When Disney World opened in Orlando, Walt Disney had already passed away, so his widow attended the dedication ceremony and represented him. They said, "We want you to come to the grand opening." The speaker at the podium who was introducing her took a long look at the tremendous crowd... he looked at the completed attractions at Disney World... and then he finally looked at Mrs. Disney and said, "Mrs. Disney, it's such a shame Walt didn't see this."

And with that, she stood up and looked at the thousands

of people and she laughed, "But, you don't understand. Walt saw this."

Again, it's the power of vision. Of course Walt Disney saw Disney World in his mind's eye as if it were already constructed.

I was at a business conference with someone who, eleven years earlier, had been a house painter making six dollars an hour. Today, he presides over a $70 million business. I was standing with somebody who laughed and said, "Who would have ever expected this." I said, "Well, I know a 6 dollar an hour house painter who did"

You see these things happen... It's vision. If we can dream it, we can do it. I have seen it happen so many times.

Charles Schwab is another modern-day visionary. It was Schwab who glimpsed the future that would result from the convergence of the Information Age with the traditional ways of investing on Wall Street. On the strength of his vision, Charles Schwab has built a financial services powerhouse offering small, individual investors the opportunity to manage their own money using the Internet.

The firm, Charles Schwab, is now the fourth largest brokerage firm in the United States. There are well more than a million on-line traders and that number is growing every day. Relatively soon, money management over the Internet will become the rule, not the exception. What was only imagined a few years ago, will have been made a reality by Charles Schwab's vision that "everyone can take control of their financial future."

Schwab, by the way, suffers from dyslexia. But he had a tremendous vision for how technology could revolutionize personal investing. Charles Schwab has created something that even George Jetson could never have conceived.

In Japanese business there has always been a great

appreciation for the importance of vision. And it's no coincidence that Japan has produced many of the most successful companies during the past 30 years — companies run by visionaries.

For example, the Sony Corporation went from a maker of cheap transistor radios to a world leader in electronic entertainment equipment. Sony's founder, Masaru Ibuka, believed that the company could only achieve greatness with a bold and compelling vision, "To create a product that becomes pervasive worldwide."

Take the Honda Corporation. In 1970, most automobile experts and consumers considered Honda to be a third-rate producer of cars. Who would have believed that, within fifteen years, Honda would be delivering more cars of higher quality than Chrysler? But it happened. The vision at Honda, and for that matter other Japanese auto makers, pushed and inspired them to develop an almost endless array of competitive strategies.

Speaking of Chrysler, it was the vision of Chairman Lee Iacocca that stared down his toughest competitors. Everyone thought that Chrysler was going to go bankrupt, but Iacocca had a different vision. He said, "Chrysler is going to be the biggest and the best."

His vision led to Chrysler producing a van that now accounts for 7 percent of all American auto sales. Clearly, Iacocca dared to dream big and then inspired people to achieve the vision he had for Chrysler.

Vision In Leadership

Vision is the basis for the best kind of leadership. Instinctively, most of us follow a leader who has real vision and who we sense can transform that vision into meaningful, effective and inspirational strategies. Vision is not simply projecting what the sales targets should be for the next quarter. Vision is not just seeing things as they are. Vision is the ability to see things as they can be.

Former Secretary of State Henry Kissinger said, "The task of the leader is to get his people from where they are to where they have not been. Leaders must invoke great vision. Those leaders who do not are ultimately judged (to be) failures."

A leader with vision embarks on voyages to new worlds. A vision looks ahead to the future and analyzes it... anticipates it. A vision, almost by definition, does not run from change as so many people do, but embraces change as absolutely essential. A leader without vision eventually loses his or her followers. An organization without vision, whether that organization is a business or a church or team or a family eventually stagnates and perhaps even wastes away.

Leaders need an ability to look through a variety of lenses. We need to look through the lens of those who follow us. We need to look through the lens of change and innovation. We need to look through the lens of our own hard experience and failure. We need to look hard at our future.

I encourage you to write a vision statement for your own life. I did, and I trace much of my success to it. So what makes a good Personal Vision Statement? A Personal Vision Statement has the following seven characteristics:

1   It is from the heart. A Personal Vision Statement should project your passions. What are you passionate about accomplishing? What do you absolutely love to do? Your vision should lead you to a place, a position in life, where you want to be more than anywhere else in the world.

2   A Personal Vision Statement should be inspirational. It needs to inspire your energies and your intellect. If a Personal Vision Statement fails to inspire you, then it probably doesn't accurately describe the destination you want to reach.

3   Your Personal Vision Statement should be simple and direct so you can readily communicate it to others who you may want to join you in your quest to fulfill your vision.

4   The Personal Vision Statement says something that applies uniquely to you. A Personal Vision Statement is not generic. It should be unique to you.

5   A Personal Vision Statement must give clear direction to you so that a year from now you can evaluate how much progress you have made toward achieving your vision.

6   A Personal Vision Statement must have staying power... it should hold up over time. A Personal Vision Statement is not like a newspaper that you read in the morning and then throw away at the end of the day. A

Personal Vision Statement will be useful to you as a guide for years to come.

7   Your Personal Vision Statement needs to be a statement that you adhere to and follow with fierce determination. It must be a statement that you are absolutely committed to. In a sense, you should be prepared to cling to your vision the way you uphold your marriage. It's "for better or worse, in sickness and in health, till death do you part." That's how strongly you should feel about your vision.

Let me try to underscore that for a moment by sharing with you a survey that I read. I think it shows a lot of different things, but more than anything, it shows a group of folks who seem to need to develop a clearer vision for their lives.

Nearly 3,000 lawyers were interviewed for this survey that appeared in TRIAL Magazine. Here's what they found. Out of 3,000 lawyers, 254 said they contemplated suicide at least two times each month... 430 said they were dissatisfied with their lives... 544 lawyers said they showed signs of depression at least 3 times a month... 963 said they felt "very lonely" or remote from other people during the previous month.

What this survey tells me is that many of these individuals don't have a vision. They're not passionate about what they're doing. They're not dreaming big. They lack significance in their lives. They're missing out on all the things that a vision will do.

Now, lets talk about sharing your vision. Once you have a personal vision, it's essential to remember how important it is to be able to communicate your vision to the men and women you may hope to lead. Think of all the visions that have gone unfulfilled because of the inability to communicate them.

The success of most entrepreneurs and business executives is driven by having a vision and their ability to communicate that vision to the men and women they hope to lead. As I said earlier, a vision can waste away without the strength and vitality of individuals supporting it. I shudder to think of how many magnificent visions have been lost because of the failure of the visionary to communicate it in a meaningful way to others.

Therefore, I want to spend a few moments talking about the importance of sharing your vision.

Business consultant and author Peter Scholtes says, "A shared vision is not an idea; it is a force in people's hearts... a force of impressive power. It fills their desire to be connected in an important undertaking."

A good idea does not qualify as a vision. There needs to be some risk attached to the idea... there needs to be some promise of change. A vision requires that you as an individual must stretch... that you and your organization are attempting to accomplish something that may seem unattainable.

Just as a skilled craftsman envisions a finished product before beginning to work, a good leader knows where he or she wants to go before moving forward or attempting to inspire others to move forward. As you can see, vision is at the very heart of good leadership. For every one person with an ambitious vision, thousands are moved to act.

Effective vision provides a context for action. Vision gives purpose and establishes meaning. Visions are clear and challenging and about excellence. A vision should be able and stable enough to stand the test of time and flexible enough to embrace change. A vision empowers other people for the future while, perhaps, having roots in the past. Remember, as Sir Isaac Newton said, "I have seen so far because I have stood on the shoulders of giants."

A vision inspires people to accomplish feats that may never before have been attempted. A strong vision replaces the fear of the unknown. Fear and resistance to change are replaced by a sense of purpose, by excitement, by desire and courage. Most of all, a vision replaces fear of the unknown with action.

Help To Build A Cathedral

To be successful, you have to think with the end in mind. Where do you want to go? Stephen Covey says, "People are in need of a vision and less in need of a road map."

Organizations without a vision may stumble along for awhile but they will never really succeed. Organizations without visions remain merely organizations. They survive, they get by, but they never move toward their real potential.

The right-shared vision provides an inspiring picture of an ideal destination shared by everyone. It is the force that drives everything in an organization. Here's what the right-shared vision will do for you and your organization.

It will motivate your people. People want work that they can believe in. They want their work to provide meaning in their lives... to be meaningful. The right-shared vision will excite people... it will make them work harder because they believe in your vision. The right-shared vision will unite people just like any championship sports team is united with a vision of winning the ultimate prize in its sport.

The right-shared vision will encourage people to take risks… to innovate… to experiment. The right-shared vision will help people overcome their fears. Most people fear the future; they fear the consequences of their decisions. But the right shared vision will actually give your people courage. Just think how valuable that is.

What all people need, regardless of their job or the kind of work they do, is a vision of what their place is and may be. They need an objective and a purpose. They need a feeling and a belief that they have some worthwhile thing to do. It's like the story of the three men who are working at a construction site. They're all doing the same job but when each man is asked what they're doing, their answers are different. The first one says, "I'm breaking rocks." The second one says, "I'm earning my living." The third one says, "I'm helping to build a cathedral." That's what vision does for you and the people you want to lead.

The right-shared vision is what drives everything in an organization. It sets a standard for people to work toward; it establishes the horizon you all want to reach. It helps individuals distinguish between what is good and bad for the organization, and what is worthwhile to achieve. It provides a context in which people can make big, important decisions about the future. Therefore, in a very practical sense, a shared vision empowers people, shapes their behavior and coordinates their efforts.

Oliver Wendell Holmes said, "Every now and then, a man's mind is stretched by a new idea or sensation and never shrinks back to its former dimensions." That's what having a vision will do for you.

For both individuals and organizations, visions are often

developed by asking a series of questions. For example, as an organization, can you become something you are not now? Does the vision give you hope or is it just a fantasy? How do you take concrete steps each day to move toward your vision? How is your organization's vision related to change and innovation? Does your vision unite your organization... inspire your people and give them purpose?

These are some of the questions you need to ask yourself. The quality of your answers will explain a lot about the quality of your organization's vision.

When you strive to accomplish great things in your life, people tell you, "You can't do it." You need to respond by thinking and speaking your success into existence. You need to keep speaking it over and over — you're going to make it... you're going to make it... you're going to make it... because you can make it as long as your dream's big enough. And it's got to be crystal clear and you've got to define it with your vision.

I tell people every day, "It's not what you want to do in your life that's important, it's what you want out of your life that's important, and you go and do whatever you have to do to get what you want in your life." As long as it's legal, as long as it's ethical, and as long as it's moral. It's got to be something big. John F. Kennedy once said, "A man may die, nations may rise and fall, but an idea lives on. Ideas have endurance without death." He was describing the power of ideas... the power of having a vision.

Earlier, I mentioned that there is no age requirement associated with having a vision for your life. You may recall the great discoverer, Magellan, who was the first captain to cross the Pacific. Virgil was considered the greatest poet in ancient Rome. Rafael was considered the "Prince of Painters,"

Chopin, the "Poet of Music." Alexander the Great was the first king to be called "Great." Wilbur Wright, who I discussed earlier, put us in a motorized plane and took us over trees. It had never been done before. These people made history. They changed the way we see the world. And every single one of them died before they were 50 years old.

All I'm trying to say is, don't wait, do something great with your life...now. And don't think you have to wait until you're 60 or 70 years old to do something great. Handel, at the age of 21, composed two operas. Mozart, at the age of 5, composed a minuet; 9, a symphony; 12, his first opera; and at 13 he was composing concertos and sonatas. Nietzsche, at the age of 14, was writing an autobiography. Isaac Newton did his greatest work before he was 25.

Alexander the Great was crowned the King of Macedonia at the age of 20. Genghis Khan at the age of 21 was called "Universal Ruler." Napoleon, in his mid-30s, was named "Emperor of Europe." Emperor of Europe. Imagine.

Most people don't realize this about Bill Gates, but he dropped out of college to pursue his vision of starting a computer software company. He was so hungry to do it that he dropped out of college. Bill Gates, the richest man in the world, is a college drop-out. But he had vision. Steven Jobs and Steve Wozniak were college kids working in the garage behind their parents' house when they founded Apple Computers. They had vision.

Bill Gates is one of the most important minds and personalities of our generation. He defeated his competitors in the world of desktop operating systems and application software. Now he's moving on to make Microsoft not only a software company but a media and content company. Bill Gates keeps pushing back the horizon of his vision of what is possible. Once he accomplishes a goal he redefines a new goal.

Let me tell you something about Bill Gates that I think you will find interesting and helpful as you work to fulfill your own vision, whatever it might be. Bill Gates has always wanted to win, he loves to win. Do you know who he learned it from? He learned it from his mother. His mom would organize card games and trivia contests when Bill Gates and his sister Mary were just kids. They would play the game Password. And they played these games very seriously. Winning mattered to Bill Gates even as a boy and it has mattered to him his entire life.

Do you know what he does now when he gets together with his original business partner, Bill Allen? Gates says, "We like to talk about how the fantasies we had as kids actually came true."

Winning matters, folks. You will achieve your vision if you pursue it in such a tenacious way that it matters to you whether you win. There are going to be a lot of times when you doubt yourself, when you don't know whether you can do it. Other people are going to doubt you. But having a vision enables you to seize control of your destiny. The vision you have for your future is your future if you have the courage to work for it.

The author Louisa May Alcott wrote, "Far away in the sunshine are my highest aspirations. I can look up and see their beauty, believe in them and try to follow them."

Eleanor Roosevelt said, "The future belongs to those who believe in the power of their dreams."

The best advice I can give you is to dare to dream. You have every right to. I'm positive that you are reading this book because you have already overcome obstacles in your life… you have had great victories and you have taken your defeats and kept going. Always remember that a person with a dream is an indomitable being. You own your dream, and you can live it. The best way to predict your future is to create it.

In a way, vision is like Mozart's melodies. The music exists on paper but it means nothing until it is both performed and heard. Much of the music's effect depends on the ability of who is playing it. Vision is like the music. It must be played to become reality.

Remember, a compelling vision is the foundation of leadership. It is absolutely essential. Nonetheless, a vision is only the foundation. It is a beginning, a starting point. It is not a destination itself.

What's important to remember about vision is that you can always do better. You can always reach higher. You can always improve. You can always innovate. Having a vision for your life is not a one-time, sudden event. It is an ongoing process.

You can do great things. Moliere said, "All men are alike in their dreams, and all men are alike in the promises they make, but the difference is in what they do." It's not what you say, it's what you do with your life that makes a big difference. Dream really big — bigger than you've ever dreamed in your life — because you can do it.

What I have observed in my life is that people usually don't want too much. What holds them back is that they want too little. They think too small. So dream big because you can live your dreams. You don't have to follow a trail that anyone else has laid out for you. Blaze your own trail so that people will follow you.

I believe in you. I believe that you can do anything. And

when somebody tells you it won't work, when somebody tells you it's never been done before, well, even if it's never been done before, you can do it. You can do it. Just tell yourself, I can win. I can win. I can win.

How you live your life will determine whether you transform your vision into reality. Your life is not the sum total of what you have been. Your life will be determined by what you yearn to become.

CHAPTER TWO
COURAGE

"It is courage, courage, courage, that raises the blood of life to crimson splendor." — George Bernard Shaw

The Latin root of the word "courage" means "heart." Courage, then, is at the heart of the matter in everything we do.

Courage is often associated with dramatic acts of heroism, and over the next few pages I will share with you some inspirational stories of heroic courage. But the kind of courage I want to discuss with you is the courage we need to have every day. The courage to deal with the challenges and decisions we face every day of our lives... the courage we need to be successful entrepreneurs and business people... the courage we need to be good husbands and wives and parents... the courage we need to be leaders in whatever profession we may choose... the courage we need to serve our communities and give something back to those who may be less fortunate than we are.

I want to discuss the type of courage we need to be winners. And I want to prove to you that you already possess the courage you need to accomplish everything you want in your life. I want to prove to you that you already have the courage inside you to accomplish greatness.

It has been said that life is not made up of a limited number of big decisions but a multitude of small ones. Our courage shows up every day in small but important ways - in ways that define who we are and how successful we will be.

Rose Kennedy, who lived to be 104 years old and who saw three of her four sons die tragically before their times, said, "Life isn't a matter of milestones, but of moments."

Dreams and vision activate our imagination and can point our lives in new, exciting, and prosperous directions. But vision without action is merely a day dream. It is courage that gives us the boldness to act, to move forward toward achieving our vision. It is courage that gives us the strength to live our lives in pursuit of victory.

I can promise you one thing. When you stand up and set yourself apart, and challenge the mediocrity around you, people are going to laugh — I guarantee it. People will laugh at you when you speak of wanting to win, of wanting more for your life and for your family. At that critical moment, the average person succumbs. When they hear the laughter, when they hear people question their vision and their goals, they retreat. They surrender. They give up without ever really getting started.

But the above-average person — the person who refuses to go through life as a nameless, faceless statistic — finds the courage to face that laughter and move on. Living your life to win means striving to achieve your goals despite what other people might say, despite the obstacles you may face. And the most beautiful part about courage is that you don't have to go looking for it — courage will find you. Courage is already inside of you. All you have to do is claim the courage that is yours.

To be courageous requires no special qualifications… no magic formula… no unique time, place or set of circumstances. Opportunities to be courageous present themselves to us all the time.

Winston Churchill wrote, "Courage is rightly esteemed the first of human qualities because it is the quality which guarantees all the others." Churchill also said, "Success is never final. Failure is never fatal. It is courage that counts." Yes, it is courage that counts.

Andrew Jackson said, "One man with courage is a majority." One man or one woman with courage becomes a majority. It takes one person to stand up to make a difference. I hear this a lot of times when people say, "But I don't know that I can make a difference."

Of course you can make a difference. And I guarantee you that you already have made a difference in the lives around you. Think about it. Researchers say that even the shyest person will influence 10,000 people during the course of their lifetime. Clearly, each and every one of us has the potential to make a large and meaningful difference in our businesses... in our families... in our communities. We can be true leaders if we find the courage to act.

Let me tell you something I admire about you. I know that by simply reading this book you are already motivated to make a difference. So remember, it takes just one person standing up and speaking their mind to take over a room. One person can take over and motivate a team. One person can take over and mobilize a company. One person can take over and lead a nation.

In battle, one soldier with courage has meant the difference between victory and defeat. A lone preacher has moved multitudes. It was one man who broke the color barrier in baseball and, by himself, helped change the face of our nation.

Elections have been decided by one vote. It was one vote in the United States Senate that saved President Andrew Johnson from impeachment. It was one vote that brought to power the ultimate mad-man, Adolf Hitler, to lead the Nazi Party in Germany. Don't ever think that one person can't or won't make a difference. You do and you will.

You see courage of all kinds in the lives and accomplishments of great people throughout history. You see one person standing up and making a difference again and again and again.

Socrates, who is considered one of the wisest men in history, had the courage not to compromise his pursuit of truth. He refused to compromise his philosophies and teachings. Socrates was brought up on false charges, convicted, and forced to commit suicide by swallowing hemlock. Plato, a student of Socrates, held courage in such high esteem that he considered it as one of the cardinal virtues.

Copernicus was laughed at when he discovered that the sun is the center of the solar system and that the earth revolves around it. Laughed at. Galileo was threatened with execution and later placed under house arrest because he actually proved that what Copernicus had discovered was true.

Great composers such as Wagner and Debussy were booed and hissed offstage. They were written off by the critics. But they kept coming back. They were courageous. And they've contributed some of the greatest music in the world.

Claude Monet was the originator of impressionism. Today, people stand in lines that stretch entire city blocks to buy tickets to see Monet paintings on exhibit in museums around the world. Claude Monet literally looked at the world differently than any artist who had come before him. And yet, one of the art critics of his day said, "Claude Monet has declared war on beauty."

You see, people laughed at him for having the courage to pursue his vision of art. But he had the courage to keep going.

And I wonder how many of us wish we had the millions of dollars to buy some of Monet's paintings.

Piscasso was the same way. He broke all the rules that artists had followed since the Renaissance. Piscasso's courage to develop his own style, his willingness to explore something new, contributed more to modern art than anyone before or since.

Look at Gregor Mendel; he was the scientist who discovered the laws of heredity. His work was ignored by the scientific community of his generation. Ignored and ridiculed. Even though Mendel was brilliant, because of a lack of money, he was forced to live as a monk to support his scientific experiments. But Mendel had courage; he kept working. And today we know that Mendel's work dramatically improved food production around the world, and his laws of heredity have been applied to biochemistry, physiology and even social science.

When Mendel was asked to discuss his efforts he said, "It requires indeed some courage to undertake labor of such far-reaching extent."

Madame Curie, another scientist, devoted her entire career to studying radioactivity and, as a result, more than one million soldiers were x-rayed with her equipment during World War I. Madame Curie died of leukemia, most likely caused by her lifelong exposure to radioactive materials.

In the mid-1800s, Joseph Lister was the first person to realize that most surgery patients did not die from the actual surgery but from infections that occurred after surgery. People in those days knew nothing about germs, and Lister's work was not accepted for years. Late in his life, Lister's findings were validated and we now know that his research turned hospitals from centers of almost certain death to centers of healing and hope. It was courage.

In fact, it was Dr. Lister who tried to save the life of the immortal English poet, Robert Ernest Henley, who wrote the poem, "Invictus." Invictus is the Latin word for "undefeated." When you study Henley's brief life, it seems that he was anything but undefeated. However, although he lived only 25 years, there are few people who ever displayed more courage than Henley.

He lived in poverty his entire life. As a child, he suffered from a painful infection of the bones, and he lived during a time when amputation was the treatment for such diseases. For the last two years of his life, he endured more than 20 operations in an attempt to save himself. Dr. Lister tried every possible remedy but Henley ultimately died in his care.

But out of the pain and suffering of his own life, and out of the courage he had in the face of his tremendous physical and financial hardships, Henley wrote one of the most emotionally powerful and uplifting poems ever written. I know several people who have a framed copy of this poem on their desk or next to their bed for inspiration. You may find it inspirational as well. Here it is:

"Out of the Night that covers me,
Black as the pit from pole to pole,
I thank whatever gods may be
For my unconquerable soul.

In the fell clutch of circumstance
I have not winced nor cried aloud.
Under the bludgeonings of chance
My head is bloodied but unbowed.

Beyond this place of wrath and tears
Looms but the Horror of the shade,
And yet the menace of the years
finds and shall find me unafraid.

It matters not how straight the gate,
How charged with punishments the scroll,
I am the master of my fate:
I am the captain of my soul.

Courage Can Build A Country

The historian, Robert McCracken, wrote, "This country was not built by men who relied on somebody else to take care of them. It was built by men who relied on themselves, who dared to shape their own lives, who had enough courage to blaze new trails — enough confidence in themselves to take the necessary risks."

A week before the Battle of Bull Run, which would mark the beginning of the Civil War, a major in the Union Army named Sullivan Ballou wrote home to his wife in Rhode Island, "Lest I should not be able to write you again, I feel compelled to write a few lines that may fall under your eye when I shall be no more. I have no misgivings about, or lack of confidence in, the cause of which I am engaged... and my courage does not halt or falter. I know how strongly American civilization now leans on the triumph of the government, and how great a debt we owe to those who came before us... And I am willing — perfectly willing — to lay down all my joys in this life to pay that debt."

Major Sullivan Ballou was killed in the Battle of Bull Run. He paid his debt to America's Founding Fathers with his life.

One of my favorite stories is about Charles Lindbergh. When Lindbergh prepared for his solo flight across the Atlantic Ocean, the famous insurance company, Lloyd's of London, refused to offer odds because the trip was too dangerous. Remember, this was in 1927. Lindbergh piloted his airplane alone for more than 33 hours before finally landing in France. I'm sure he felt fear at some point during every single one of those hours but he kept going. And when he landed, he was proclaimed a hero in every corner of the world.

Perhaps the quintessential American moment of courageous leadership occurred about six years after Lindbergh's flight. In March of 1933, the United States was in the worst depression of its history. The economic life of the nation had slowed to an almost complete standstill. An estimated 15 million men were unemployed. Their families were hungry and cold. Many of them were homeless. Hundreds of thousands of farmers had lost their land. Banks were closing... factories were closing... and people were in a state of anxiety that bordered on desperation. Fear hung like a heavy cloud over the entire nation.

Against this backdrop of national depression and fear, a new President was being inaugurated on the 4th of March. The nation awaited his address, which would be his first formal message to the people. Thousands of men and women jammed the space in front of the east steps of the Capitol building in Washington where he was to speak. Millions of people across the nation waited beside their radios wondering what the new President would say. They wondered what he could say to ease the dread in their hearts and give them hope for the future.

Franklin Delano Roosevelt stood and faced the huge, hushed crowd. He was conscious of his role on this fateful day, of the problems he faced, and his great responsibility to the people and to the nation. He was assuming the highest office in the land, amid the throes of a crisis unprecedented in times of peace. He knew there was hardly a home in America that had not been affected by the depression to some degree... he knew that fear held the nation in its demoralizing grip... and that his first task was to restore confidence and courage among the American people.

Roosevelt said, "This is a day of national consecration."

His voice rang out, firm and clear, reaching to the far limits of the crowd. It echoed in millions of homes across the land, dynamic and compelling. This was no time for evasion, he told the people. This was a time to speak out boldly, to face the facts. There were grave problems ahead, but he asked the people to meet the challenge with courage, to have faith in the nation and its future. He said, "This great nation will endure as it has endured, will revive and will prosper. So first of all, let me assert my firm belief that the only thing we have to fear is fear itself — nameless, unreasoning, unjustified terror which paralyzes needed efforts to convert retreat into advance."

There was an electric quality to his words, to his voice. All over the country people relaxed as they listened. His vigor, his assurance, his vast optimism about the future, had their effect; and hope returned to the hearts of literally millions of Americans.

FDR spoke with courage. The words he used were brave words. And he re-kindled the great American spirit by reminding us to use our own, individual courage. We did not have to fear anything.

Another great story of facing and overcoming fear with courage is that of Martin Luther King, Jr. He held on to his beliefs even though he was attacked... even though he was imprisoned... even though his house was bombed on three different occasions. He held the courage of his convictions and he never backed down. Martin Luther King, Jr. taught us what it was like to have the courage to stand up for what we believe in, in a dignified, nonviolent way.

Taking Risks

Having courage means that sometimes you have to be willing to take risks. Do you remember Christa McAuliffe, the high school teacher from New Hampshire who volunteered to join the Space Shuttle Challenger crew in 1985? She showed us real courage.

Christa McAulliffe was a woman who was willing to venture out into the unknown in the space shuttle. She risked her life... she ultimately lost her life in the pursuit of knowledge. She wanted to go into space because that's where the future is, and she wanted to tell her students about it. She never got a chance to do that. But Christa McAuliffe did show us something very powerful — that sometimes to grow, to move forward, we have to risk something. Her motto was "Reach for the stars." Christa McAuliffe taught us all that ordinary people, each and every one of us, possess extraordinary courage if we will just use it.

In the end, Christa McAuliffe taught us about courage and grace, and she reminded us that it's a good and fine thing to serve your country, and to serve the pursuit of knowledge.

What a moving life she led, and what tremendous courage she showed us.

When First Lady Betty Ford was still in the White House, she was diagnosed with breast cancer after what was supposed to be a routine doctor's appointment. A day later, Betty Ford underwent surgery where doctors found that her cancer had spread badly enough in one breast that they had to remove it.

This was back in the mid-1970s when breast cancer was seldom discussed, and millions of women went year after year without proper breast examinations. Betty Ford could have remained silent about her own tragedy but she was courageous enough to tell her story in the hope that it would help protect other women. It took great courage on her part to share this personal and painful experience with the world.

Betty Ford was courageous enough to sacrifice her own privacy to save other women. She made a difference.

Let me tell you another story about the courage of someone to stand up to cancer. Terry Fox was a terrific Canadian athlete who lettered in several sports in college and was looking forward to the possibility of becoming a professional athlete. One day he started having trouble with his leg and went to a doctor. He found out that he had cancer. It was ravaging his leg. The doctor said, "I'm sorry, but we have to amputate your leg. Since you're 21 years old, you have to sign the approval forms allowing us to do that."

During the next several days, after the operation, as he was recovering in his hospital room, Terry did not dwell on his loss as you might expect. He was disheartened that his athletic career was over before it had really gotten started, but he found himself lying in his hospital bed thinking, "You can do anything — if you do it with your whole heart."

Terry decided that he wanted to run from one end of Canada to the other. His goal would be to raise $100,000 and donate it to a youth cancer research facility so that he could prevent other young people from suffering the same pain and torment he had endured. He wrote down his goal and thought about it constantly.

Once he was released from the hospital, Terry was fitted with a prosthesis, or false leg. He started getting used to it… he hobbled around and told people about his plans to organize "Terry Fox's Marathon of Hope." He went to his mom and dad and told them what it was he wanted to do.

His father said, "Look, son, we saved our money and it's available to you — if you decide to go back to college. Once you graduate, then you can go and make a contribution." The next day Terry went to the Canadian Cancer Society and announced his intention of raising money through a marathon. The Cancer Society officials told him they would have to put it on a back burner because they were involved with a lot of other activities. They said his parents were right. "Skip it for now. Come back and see us again another time. But thank you for thinking of it."

The very next day, he went to school and talked his college roommate into dropping out. The two of them flew out to Newfoundland. That's where Terry dropped his crutch into the Atlantic Ocean and began his cross-country run westward.

At first, no one really noticed what Terry was doing. The media paid him little attention. His prosthesis caused the stump of his leg to bleed. Still, he slowly increased his daily mileage until he was running 31 miles — more than a marathon a day!

After more than 300 days of running, Terry got to meet the Prime Minister of Canada. They shook hands and Prime

Minister Trudeau asked him what he was really trying to accomplish. Terry said his original goal was to raise $100,000, but with the Prime Minister's assistance, he could expand that goal to $1 million. At first, Prime Minister Trudeau demurred; he didn't want to get involved.

At about this time, the U.S. media began to pick up on Terry's story. Celebrities like hockey player Wayne Gretzky got involved and the money started to pour in.

Terry kept on running. He got all the way to Ontario when he started to develop serious respiratory problems. He went to see a doctor and the doctor told him, "You need to stop your run."

Terry told the doctor that he didn't know who he was talking to. Terry said, "In the beginning, my parents told me I couldn't do it, but I chose to go ahead anyway. The Cancer Society told me "no thanks" and I chose to go on. The local governments told me to stop because I was clogging the highways. I chose to go ahead. The Prime Minister didn't really want to support me after I got $100,000, but finally he got behind it and we raised a million. When I leave your office, I plan to collect one dollar for every living Canadian — $24.1 million."

The doctor replied that he sincerely wished that Terry could finish his run, but he explained that the cancer had spread throughout his chest. He explained to Terry that he had become a national hero. He told him that there was a Canadian Air Force jet waiting at the runway to fly him home to Vancouver, where his parents would be waiting to take him to the hospital. Reluctantly, Terry agreed.

Terry went home and actually survived for another few years. Once, as his condition worsened and he was being rolled into the emergency room on a gurney, a young reporter asked, "Terry, what are you going to do next?"

Terry was courageous until the very end. He looked into the camera and challenged the people watching TV at home, "Are you going to finish my run? Are you going to finish my run?"

He died a short time later. Ultimately, Canadians did raise $24.1 million for Terry Fox's cancer research fund. It took vision for Terry to imagine his run across Canada. It took perseverance for him to keep going. But it took courage for him to take the first step. And look what he accomplished.

Terry Fox's first step was to overcome his fear — his fear about his disease and his fear of the journey ahead of him. But we all face fear. It's what we do in response to fear that counts.

There Is No Courage Without Fear

I grew up in Virginia, just across the Potomac River from Washington, DC. My father has worked years for Senator Strom Thurmond, the longest serving Senator in history. During my life, I have been honored to meet and talk with military heroes who have served our nation during wartime. I always ask them about their courage because we all assume that, as soldiers, they are so brave.

It's amazing what I've learned from these war heroes. During interviews I have asked them if they were afraid. I think we are all curious about this. Most of them say without hesitation that, of course, they were. And sometimes you want to sit and say, "Not you! You weren't that afraid." They say, "I was more afraid than anybody else out there. That's how I responded to my fear."

Fear is a critical part of courage. You have a choice. When faced with an obstacle you attack it or you run from it. And it's amazing, when you attack it they pin medals on you, they put you up at the head table and ask you to give speeches. And yet you're still afraid. That's okay because everyone is afraid. But what separates you from other people is how you respond to your fear.

One thing I'd like to emphasize with you is that as you move through life you are going to be afraid. You're going to be scared before you become a parent; you're going to be scared as you raise your kids. You're going to be scared when you accept a new job or when you accept a new challenge at your current job. You're going to be scared when you get promoted to the next level. You're going to be climbing the ladder, you're going to move up higher and higher and you're going to wonder, "Am I up to it? Am I good enough? Am I a good enough leader? I hope I don't let anybody down. I hope nobody sees how scared I am."

You're going to be scared before making business presentations. You're going to be scared to make a cold call or to show someone your business plan. You know what? Everybody is. Everybody gets scared. It doesn't matter. Do it anyway.

When my wife Sandy and I were building our business, we used to lay awake at night and talk about some of our fears. We all have fears about certain things in our lives. But Sandy and I faced them… we talked them through. We found the courage to take the steps each day that would lead to having a successful and thriving business.

Recently I heard an amazing statistic; maybe you are familiar with it. On the West Coast, in the area from Menlo Park north to Seattle, there are now 120 technology-based companies that have a stock market value above $1 billion apiece. That's not combined, each one of them is above $1 billion in value. Very few of them even existed 10 years ago. Obviously, every one of the founders of these companies had enough courage to overcome their fears and create something great. What I believe from the bottom of my heart is very simple. So do you. So do you. You have the same courage as these entrepreneurs, or maybe even more courage.

The Russian poet and novelist Boris Pasternak said talent and the art of writing is defined as "boldness in the face of a blank sheet of paper." That's courage. It's having the will to write your first word... the will to take your first step, or your next step... it's the will to overcome your fear of failure.

Success in almost any endeavor requires bold decision-making and a willingness to take informed risks. A researcher at Princeton University recently said, "An excessive zeal to avoid all risks is, in the end, an acceptance of mediocrity and an abdication of leadership." In everything you do, you must be willing to take on the toughest challenge and view it as the greatest opportunity.

I love what Teddy Roosevelt said about having the will to face tough challenges. He said, "Far better it is to dare mighty things, to win glorious triumphs even though checkered by failure, than to rank with those poor spirits who neither enjoy nor suffer much because they live in the gray twilight that knows neither victory nor defeat." Dare to do mighty things because, with courage, you can and will do mighty things.

A school teacher was once quoted as saying, "A great idea will come to you three times. If you go with it the first time, it will do nearly all the work for you. Even if you don't move until the second time, it will still do half the work for you. But if you leave it until the third time, you will have to do all the work yourself." It's a matter of having the courage to follow your great ideas. Follow your great ideas in spite of your fears.

When you're scared all that means is that you really care about what you're doing. It means you want to succeed. It means that it is meaningful to you. And it means that if you can overcome your fear and just keep going, you are probably going to succeed. That's what courage is.

My wife has a great way of looking at fear. She uses humor to deal with it. It's amazing because, when you think about it, she's absolutely right. Sandy says, "Don't be afraid of anything unless it can eat you." Now people always laugh at that, but it's true. Don't be afraid of anything unless it can eat you. Remember that when you are getting ready for an important meeting. You'll feel a lot better.

The advice columnist, Ann Landers, once said, "If I were asked to give what I consider the single most useful bit of advice it would be this, 'Expect trouble as an inevitable part of life and when it comes, hold your head high, look it squarely in the eye and say, *I will be bigger than you. You cannot defeat me.*'"

You cannot defeat me. Jackie Joyner-Kersee, the world's greatest female athlete during the past decade, did not let trouble defeat her. She was born into poverty in the public housing projects of East St. Louis. At 11, she witnessed a murder in front of her own home. At 12, her grandmother was shot and killed. At 19, she lost her mom to a sudden attack of meningitis. Later that same year, Jackie herself was diagnosed with asthma.

Jackie could have easily viewed herself as a victim. She could have easily taken her life in a completely different direction. She could have settled for mediocrity and mere survival. Everyone would have understood. No one would have criticized her for that.

But Jackie Joyner-Kersee was too courageous for that. She wanted to beat the odds of having been born and raised in a ghetto.

During her 15-year career in track and field, Jackie has won three Olympic gold medals, one silver and one bronze. She is actually proudest of the bronze medal because she won it in the long jump despite a debilitating hamstring injury. She holds the world and Olympic records in the heptathlon, and the American record for the long jump, the 50-meter hurdles and the 60-meter hurdles.

We know of Jackie's brilliance as an athlete because her accomplishments have been broadcast worldwide. She has been called "a walking Platonic ideal" — a perfect fusion of speed, grace, strength and skill.

But the most moving thing about Jackie is what is in her heart and soul. She once said, "I read a lot of poetry and I believe that dreams can come true. I believe I can do anything I put my mind to. I set goals and I believe I have the capabilities to reach those goals. Something within me just tells me to move, that I can do it. I want to give people the courage and determination so they can change their lives. But I also tell them, 'Don't follow in my footsteps. Make your own.'"

Make your own footsteps. You can do it. You can do it with courage.

Let me share with you what some great people have said over the years about overcoming fear.

The author Mark Twain said, "Courage is resistance to fear, mastery of fear — not the absence of fear."

The writer Dorothy Bernard said, "Courage is fear that has said its prayers."

Henry Ford said, "Obstacles are those frightful things you

see when you take your eyes off your goals."

Walt Disney said, "All our dreams can come true if we have the courage to pursue them."

And perhaps Franklin Roosevelt said it best: "We have nothing to fear but fear itself." Confront your fears and you can make them disappear.

So you see, courage is a matter of taking action in spite of our fear. The most important battles you will ever fight are within your own heart. In your quiet moments, courage will find you. So be larger than whatever challenge you may face.

Action Conquers Fear

To be successful in any endeavor, you must be willing to act. In business... in marketing and sales... in government... in school... in your own home, you need the courage to act. To buy, sell, borrow, loan... to speak up and to move on. Having the courage to act gives you the opportunity to succeed.

I have observed in my own businesses that people fail because they are afraid to act. So, please, do not be afraid of attempting something great in your life because you may fail. Of course you may fail! But without the attempt, failure is certain!

What separates the founders of Fortune 500 companies or, for that matter, the founders of Inc. Magazine's list of the top 500 small companies from the millions of Americans who dream of starting their own companies but never do?

Well, first and foremost, when they saw a great idea staring them in the face, they didn't blink. They acted. They didn't wait for all the doubts to sink in... they didn't listen to their friends say, "Well, I don't think you should risk it"... they never allowed the endless stream of what-ifs to delay them.

The single greatest difference between those who only think and those who actually do, and this is a multi-million dollar difference, is the courage to act. When someone has the courage to start a business, they don't allow themselves to utter the word failure. They seek out advice. They write a plan. They stop eating out at restaurants and put their money away. They look for financing and if the first or the second or the third bank says "no" they keep going to the fourth and the fifth and the sixth bank if necessary. They talk to potential customers. By talking, they make it real.

Time is of the essence. People with the courage to act develop a sense of urgency. They realize we all have such a limited time that there is no time to waste.

Roberto Goizueta joined Coca-Cola as a technician in Havana in 1954. His father loaned him the money to buy 100 of the company's shares for $8,000. When Goizueta and his wife fled Fidel Castro's takeover, the only wealth he had in America was his Coke shares at Citibank in new York City. Last year, when Goizueta passed away, he had worked his way up to become the Chairman of the Coca-Cola Company. He had helped build Coke's market share from $4 billion to $164 billion. And for him, it all started with one act of courage.

Look at Josh Smith, the founder and chairman of Maxima. He said, "I didn't have the money to go out and take business courses, so I figured I'd just better learn on the job." He studied and watched and learned and then one day he quit his regular job to become an entrepreneur... to start out on his own.

He had the courage to take the risk. He could have fallen

flat on his face but he didn't. From one employee — Josh Smith - his company has grown to more than $60 million a year in sales and more than 2,000 employees. It's having the courage to take the risk to reap the rewards.

Risk and reward is the American success story. It is the American way. And it is driven by daily acts of courage - as parents... as entrepreneurs... as investors... as government officials... in every endeavor of our lives.

Be Willing To Make Some Waves

I'm not a sailor myself, but a lot of my friends are. There is a technique in small-boat sailing that is an appropriate metaphor for the need to be willing to take risks. When fog prevents a small-boat sailor from seeing the buoy marking the course he wants, he turns his boat rapidly in small circles. What this does is create waves that will rock the buoy in the vicinity. Then the sailor stops, listens and repeats the procedure until he hears the buoy clang. By making waves, the sailor finds where his course lies.

The price of finding these types of guides for our life is the willingness to take a few risks... to "make a few waves," if you will. A captain who keeps his boat in the harbor never encounters danger, but he also never gets anywhere. It takes courage to sail your boat out of its harbor. It takes courage to face the risks that will ultimately reward you.

Americans start more than one million new businesses every year, businesses which in turn create more than three-quarters of all new jobs. America is the land of opportunity. Courage is the force that creates those opportunities.

Dr. Norman Vincent Peale used to tell a great story about

a young man eager to get a job during the depression. He read a want ad that fit his abilities perfectly. He ran down to the company where the job interviews were being conducted. The problem was he found 37 people ahead of him in line.

The easiest thing to do at that point would have been to turn and walk away. Or he could have simply stood in line and probably been turned away. But instead, he wrote a note and handed it to a secretary to give to the executive who was conducting the interview. The note said simply, "Please don't hire anyone until you interview person #38, James Henry."

He went back in line. A few moments later the boss came out and walked down the line to him. He said, "Creativity and initiative are what I'm looking for. James, you're hired."

Oprah Winfrey, in a commencement speech at Spelman College, said, "Dare to be different. Be a pioneer. Be a leader. Be the kind of person who in the face of adversity will continue to embrace life and walk fearlessly toward the challenge."

Helen Keller said, "Life is either a daring adventure or nothing at all." So, please people, have the courage to make your life a daring adventure.

Do not be onlookers. As Francis Bacon wrote, it is "left only to God and to the angels to be lookers on." Do not be a spectator of your own life. Get in the game. Be involved. Take action. Excel. Be worthy of your heritage. The courage of those who went before us in this land exists in you.

Remember, the poet Robert Ernest Henley wrote, "It matters not how straight the gate... How charged with punishments the scroll... I am the master of my fate... I am the captain of my soul."

The stories of courageous men and women throughout history can help define what courage is. These stories can help demonstrate courage, sometimes in dramatic ways. They can offer hope and they can provide inspiration. But they cannot supply courage itself. To find your own courage... and to use your courage to live a winning life, you must look within your own soul.

Sam Johnson is a true profile in courage. He was a POW for seven years in Vietnam. When I hear stories of people like him, I can barely even imagine what he must have endured.

As a prisoner of war, Sam Johnson endured unspeakable torture, lived in primitive conditions and suffered from malnutrition. For two of those seven years in captivity, he was imprisoned in what was known as the Hanoi Hilton. That was the worst prison camp in Vietnam. It was there that he endured the worst of his torture.

Communications between the prisoners was forbidden at the Hanoi Hilton, but that didn't stop the Americans from developing an intricate tap code that helped the prisoners maintain their sanity. Once, when Johnson and Commander James Stockdale were caught using this tap code, the Vietnamese retaliated with the worst kind of punishment. They put Johnson in a cell about two and half feet wide by eight feet long. Johnson was put into stocks so tight that he couldn't even move. The Vietnamese kept Johnson in that cell, in those stocks, for 72 days. On the 72nd day, a typhoon struck the Hanoi Hilton. Water flooded his cell. As the water kept rising higher and higher, he thought for sure that he would drown.

So he prayed. He prayed that night like he had never prayed before, and when he woke the next morning, he discovered he had survived. Not only had he survived, but the typhoon had blown the boards off his cell, and he saw the sun for the first time in 72 days. Not too long after that, Sam

Johnson boarded an airplane and returned home with 738 other American prisoners of war. Every one of them had extraordinary courage — a type of courage that should be an inspiration to us as we face challenges that are so much easier and more routine.

Facing Your Fears Takes Practice

Courage is actually born and developed by facing fear. You will develop courage through repetition and practice. Courage is nonexistent if not for fear. It is born through facing our fears. If you learn to face your fears, then it becomes easier to overcome them. As you become more practiced at overcoming your fears, your courage grows and your fears diminish. Eventually, you can look back at some of your old fears and actually laugh at them.

Perhaps the best way to develop courage is through repetition. Earlier, I discussed war heroes who privately admitted to being afraid during military battles just as we fear battles in our own lives. But, through repeatedly facing their fears, they overcome them. One of my favorite anecdotes that demonstrates this involves General George S. Patton. He had fear but he could control it.

During World War II he wrote to a friend, "It is rather interesting how you get used to death. I have had to go to inspect the troops every day, in which case you run a very good chance — or I should say a reasonable chance - of being bombed or shot at from the air, and shelled or shot at from the ground.

"I had the same experience every day, which is for the

first half hour the palms of my hands sweat and I feel very depressed. Then, if one hits near you, it seems to break the spell and you don't notice them anymore. Going back in the evenings over the same ground and at a time when the shelling and bombing is usually heavier, you become so used to it you never think about it."

Patton got so used to the possibility of dying that, once when an enemy pilot tried to shoot down the aircraft Patton was traveling in, the General actually pulled out his camera and began taking pictures. After surviving the attack, Patton wrote, "I decided I might as well take some pictures of my impending demise. There wasn't anything to do, so I thought I might as well use the camera. But after it was all over, I found I had been so nervous I had forgotten to take the cover off the lens."

We don't have to be a five-star general to know what courage is. Developing courage is a matter of repetition. With practice, the courage to act becomes routine.

Think of the courage you have already demonstrated in your life. The very challenges you have experienced and overcome in getting this far is exactly what equips you to go farther. You have had to show flexibility, resourcefulness, diligence and grit to get wherever you are today. And those are precisely the qualities that are most valued in the world. They are all part of the courage we need to live to win.

You have faced risks growing up. You have faced risks in your career. The risk of failure looms large for all of us. You may have had to overcome poverty or a broken home or a disability or drugs and violence. Maybe you're still overcoming them even today. The fact that you are reading this means that you are willing to overcome the challenges that you have faced. You didn't give up. You took the risk, and you prevailed. It took courage. And perhaps you are preparing to take a new, even more significant risk that will require even more courage. Do it. Because you can do it. I believe in you.

The PBS evening news reporter, Jim Lehrer, says, "Take risks, be willing to put your mind and your spirit, your time and your energy, your stomach and your emotions on the line. To search for a safe place, to search for an end to the rainbow, is to search for a place that you will hate once you find it. The soul must be nourished along with the bank account and the resume. The best nourishment for any soul is to create your own risks."

The author Robert Louis Stevenson wrote, "The world has no room for cowards. We must all be ready somehow to toil, to suffer, to die. And yours is not the less noble because no drum beats before you when you go out into your daily battlefields... and no crowds shout about your coming when you return from your daily victory or defeat."

So be courageous. Claim the courage that is yours. It's inside you. Be courageous today. Courage will give life to your visions. Courage will help you win. You can do it. You can do it. You must do it.

CHAPTER THREE
PERSEVERANCE

"I am only one, but I am one. I cannot do everything, but I can do something. What I can do, I should do and, with the help of God, I will do! — Everett Hale

In Chapter One, I discussed the importance of having a vision for your life. In Chapter Two, I explored the need to have the courage to pursue your vision. In this chapter, we will explore how perseverance will enable you to overcome obstacles and adversity so that you are always moving forward in fulfillment of your vision.

The dictionary defines perseverance as "the persistent adherence to a single course of action in the face of any and all obstacles." I suppose that's the technically correct way to explain what perseverance is — the persistent adherence to a single course of action.

But here is how I would say it. Keep going. Don't stop. Keep working. Keep dreaming. Don't quit. Work some more. Don't ever, ever give up. You should expect failure after failure before you succeed, but if you never give up, then you will ultimately prevail. You will succeed.

One reason I am so passionate about perseverance is because I believe the lack of it to be the Number One Killer of dreams in the world today.

Calvin Coolidge said, "Nothing will take the place of persistence. Talent will not, nothing is more common than unsuccessful people with talent. Genius will not, unrewarded genius is almost a proverb. Education will not, the world is full of educated derelicts. Persistence, perseverance and dedication are omnipotent."

Perseverance is the key.

The people who persevere know one thing, they know they want to win... they know they want to succeed... they know they want to make it. They don't just want to survive; they don't just want to be comfortable and get by. They want significance in their lives. They want to do something great, something new for their company, something meaningful for their family, something truly worthwhile with what little time we all share.

Thomas Fuller said, "An invincible determination can accomplish almost anything and in this lies the great distinction between great men and little men."

The football coach, Mike Ditka, who led the Chicago Bears to their only Super Bowl victory says, "You are never a loser until you quit trying."

Rick Mears, the five-time winner of the Indianapolis 500 says, "To finish first you must first finish." It's perseverance.

I hear kids being taught, "It doesn't matter whether you win or lose, it's how you play the game." You know, that's a nice thought. But I don't buy it. Here's what the great American industrialist, Andrew Carnegie, thought about winning. He said, "The first man gets the oyster, the second man gets the shell."

Of course, how you play the game is critical. How you play the game says everything about your character. You must play the game with integrity. You must be honest and play by the rules.

But the reality is that it does matter whether you win or lose. It makes a difference. Life is too short. It goes by too quickly. It's not just about doing something, it's about doing it well. It's not just about playing the game of life. It's about living your life to win. It makes a difference.

There was a survey done by the National Dry Goods Association. The people doing the study wanted to measure perseverance and here's what they found: 48 percent of salespeople make one phone call and stop... 25 percent make two calls and stop... 15 percent make three calls and stop... 12 percent make three calls and keep moving forward.

Nearly half of salespeople stop at the end of one call. But do you know what? Those 12 percent who keep going make 80 percent of all the sales.

I'll tell you something about those people in the 12 percent —they want to win... they want to win... they want success... they don't just want to survive... they want significance, they want something great... something great for their company... something great for their family, something great for their organization.

Lee Iacocca, the former Chairman of Chrysler, said, "There ain't no free lunches in this country. And don't go spending your whole life commiserating that you got raw deals. You've got to say, 'I think that if I keep working at this and want it bad enough I can have it.' It's called perseverance."

You are probably familiar with the phrase, "It's a grind." You may have even used that phrase in your life to describe a tough day at the office or a punishing practice in sports or a difficult day with your kids. It's a grind.

Well, for some people, life can be a grind. But we get to decide whether the challenges that all of us invariably face every day will grind us down or actually polish us up. The people with perseverance actually get polished by their experiences... they get seasoned... they move on and move up. They're the ones who are in the 12 percent group… they're the ones making the extra call to close the deal.

You see, it matters whether you have the will to win. It makes a difference. Sandy and I were in a plane crash in 1996. It made a big difference in our lives that our pilot wanted to win. Not long ago I saw a commercial airline pilot interviewed after an emergency landing. There were tears in his eyes as he looked into the camera. The reporter who interviewed him asked him what he had been thinking about in the air. The pilot said, "I decided that this was not how it was going to end… there's going to be more… this wasn't going to be the end of it. I wasn't going to leave my wife this way."

Here's another way of looking at it. Can you imagine going in for surgery and they're wheeling you into the operating room and the surgeon grabs your hand and says, "Well, you know, it doesn't really matter whether you win or lose… I'll try… we'll just have to see what happens."

Absolutely not. You want your surgeon to look you in the eye and say, "Listen, you can count on me. We're going to win. You're going to be all right"

You can bet that I'm going to teach my daughter, Taylor, what it's like to want to win as she gets old enough to understand. Perhaps the most fundamental example of perseverance is when a young child first begins to learn to walk. Taylor went through this. When babies are first learning to walk they toddle around and fall on their bottoms again and again and again. Hundreds of times every single day. Do you know what Taylor does when she lands on her fanny? She giggles… she thinks its the funniest thing.

Now, as we get older, why do so many people lose this quality of trying to take bold, new steps? Why is it that so many people view a temporary setback as permanent? What would happen to my daughter, Taylor, if she decided on the fifth or the hundredth or the thousandth time that she fell down that she would no longer try to walk?

Why is it that babies keep trying until they actually walk? It's perseverance. They know they can do it because they see other people doing it. Eventually as children get older we can teach them to try things that no one else has ever done before.

It's perseverance that keeps us moving forward... keeps us moving up... keeps us moving toward achieving our goals. Abraham Lincoln said, "I am a slow walker, but I never walk backward." It's perseverance. In business... in sales... in teaching and learning... in politics... in sports... in everything. It's perseverance.

There Will Always Be "Circumstances"

Everyone, every organization, is confronted with adversity. Everyone faces problems, sometimes significant problems. Everyone makes mistakes, sometimes big ones.

It's relatively easy to predict that on any given day we will confront difficulties. What is less easy to predict, however, is this: What do we do when these problems arise? How do we react? Some people stop. They give up. But some people overcome repeated disappointments and setbacks.

The important thing is not the circumstances in which we find ourselves. The key is how we view these circumstances.

Napoleon said, "The greatest attribute of a soldier is not loyalty, it's not courage, it's endurance." It's endurance. It's being willing to stand up one more time, to do it one more time, to extend yourself one more time. So many people fail, they fail five times and they stop, when the sixth time they could have made it.

Ross Perot, the multimillionaire businessman, says, "Most people give up when they're about to achieve success. They quit on the one-yard line. They give up at the last minute of the game, one foot from the winning touchdown."

The great inventor, Thomas Edison, who developed the first light bulb, said, "Many of life's failures are people who did not realize how close they were to success when they gave up."

History has shown that the most notable winners are people who encountered heartbreaking obstacles. But they did not stop. They triumphed. They won because they refused to get discouraged by their defeats. History is rich with stories of perseverance.

When Van Gogh couldn't afford to buy paint brushes he made them. Beethoven wrote many of his greatest works after he had gone deaf. He kept writing beautiful music even though he could no longer hear it except in his own mind.

It has been said that as Michelangelo was working on painting the Sistine Chapel, he wouldn't eat, he wouldn't sleep, he wouldn't bathe and he would barely rest. During the night, he worked by candlelight. He had scaffolding built so he could paint on his back looking up at his work. He had a mattress sent up the scaffolding so that he could take short naps and never leave his work. Michelangelo's work on the Sistine Chapel lasted more than three years and he did it with hardly any assistance from other artists.

During the middle of the project, the Pope at the time stopped paying him. But he kept working... he kept painting.

They said that he worked so long until he finished that when he actually went to take his socks off, his skin came off in his socks. Can you imagine? Now that's perseverance!

Louis Pasteur, the scientist who invented the process of pasteurization to keep food from spoiling, lived by the motto, "Will, work and success." He believed that the willingness to persevere would help him accomplish anything he set out to do. Perseverance. It was Louis Pasteur, more than a century ago, who laid the foundation for modern medicine.

It took Noah Webster 36 years to write his dictionary. It took Gibbon 26 years to write "The Rise and Fall of the Roman Empire." Johann Gutenberg, the man who invented moveable type, worked for decades to develop his printing press. Plato wrote the first line to "The Republic," nine times. Nine times, and he hadn't even started yet. Could you imagine, you sit down — nine times and you haven't even started. But it took him nine times just to get started. Sometimes when you approach things in life it's going to take you time after time just to get started. Well, get started. And then finish.

John Wooden, the former basketball coach who created a UCLA dynasty: says, "It's not so important who starts the game, but who finishes it."

Finish what you start. Perseverance enables you to win.

Without Perseverance There Is No Survival

Winston Churchill said, "Victory at all costs. Victory in spite of all terror. Victory, however long and hard the road may be, for without victory there is no survival."

Churchill faced many long and hard roads himself. He

made numerous mistakes and faced many failures during his long public career, but he came back famously again and again and again. As we all know, it was Churchill who helped rally his nation and the entire free world to help win World War II.

America's own Founding Fathers were men of vision, great courage and character. But none of their dreams and talents would have amounted to much if they had not persevered. Major National Greene, who was General George Washington's closest and most trusted advisor during the Revolutionary War, said, "We fight, we get beat, we rise and we fight again." Washington himself said, "I trust the experience of error will enable us to act better in the future." Indeed, the birth of America is the story of perseverance.

I remember reading an analogy that drives this point home. George Washington, at a critical time during our Revolutionary War, was trying to find a way to bring his soldiers together. They weren't fighting as Americans. He was trying to win a war with people who weren't even fighting as Americans. They were fighting as Virginians and Hampshiremen and Marylanders. They were fighting for colonies' rights that they believed in, but they weren't pulling together yet as Americans. One night in the freezing cold when they hadn't eaten he said something insignificant. He said, "Let only Americans stand watch this night." Simple. Insignificant words. "Let only Americans stand watch this night." Yet it was those insignificant words that gave breath to the Declaration of Independence.

In 1963, Martin Luther King, Jr. stood on the steps of the Lincoln Memorial and gave one of the most eloquent speeches in the history of this nation, and during that speech he quoted from that same Declaration of Independence that years earlier, at a very insignificant moment, one man said, "Let only Americans stand watch this night."

In 1989 at Tiananmen Square, China, young kids were shot dead by their own people. Risking their lives for freedom, when they rolled them over to cart them away, in their hands was clenched the Declaration of the United States, the Declaration of Independence. And years earlier it seemed so insignificant, "Let only Americans stand watch this night."

What you are doing may seem insignificant but... it's not. Perseverance. Perseverance is born through seemingly insignificant moments. But they make a difference, a big difference. Marriages fail if you're not willing to persevere. Businesses fail if you don't persevere. Nations fail if their leaders do not persevere.

When you are faced with troubles, fight through them. Vow to stand tough and get through them. And when you win, you will not only have triumphed for yourself, but you will also have won the respect of your friends. And you will deserve that respect.

Perseverance is nurtured in quiet moments. Because you are usually lonely when you have to nurture it. Often when it's time to persevere it's because other people have quit. You're alone. When it's time to move on it's because other people have quit. And it's very lonely, because what you're doing feels insignificant. Once you learn to adapt to that, you realize it's not insignificant even though it feels like it at the time. Get through it, fight through it.

As I was building my companies, perseverance was the quality that got me over the hump. Perseverance was the toughest thing for me. There were many nights, many times when I was driving alone at night, when I felt like giving up. Sandy and I used to talk about it. We knew that a lack of perseverance would have killed our best efforts. So we just kept going. We simply did not ever give up. And, today, our business is exactly what we dreamed it would become when we were pouring our blood, sweat and tears into it.

Earlier in this century, President Franklin Delano Roosevelt, the only President ever to be elected to four terms, showed us what it means never to give up. He reached his goals and his dreams despite being crippled by polio. In fact, his perseverance enabled him to create the foundation that led to Jonas Salk developing the vaccine for polio.

FDR drew strength from his own disability. Roosevelt led our nation through two great crises - first, the Great Depression and then World War II. He accomplished so much in his life and so much for our country because he kept bouncing back, he never gave up.

W. Clement Stone, the multimillionaire and former Chairman of the Aeon Corporation in Chicago, said, "Every negative event contains within it the seed of an equal or greater benefit."

Let me tell you about another modern-day success story. A success story written by perseverance. This individual grew up in a tough neighborhood in New York City where drugs and crime were constant temptations. He was the son of immigrants from Jamaica. His father worked as a shipping clerk; his mother was a seamstress. His family certainly was not rich.

Growing up, he worked hard. At age 17, he took a job in a soft-drink bottling plant, where he earned 90 cents an hour mopping acres and acres of cement floors until his back ached. And throughout his life he felt the sting of racism but he kept telling himself to push forward... to work harder... not to be distracted by those who might be prejudiced. He went through college in the ROTC training program and after graduation he went to fight in Vietnam.

He came home and enrolled in graduate school. He continued his military career. With each new assignment he impressed his superiors with his hard work and diligence. He eventually landed a job as the National Security Advisor to the President. A few years later, Colin Powell was appointed Chairman of the Joint Chiefs of Staff, the highest ranking member of the military next to the Commander in Chief himself. General Powell became not only the first minority to hold that esteemed position, he was also the youngest ever to do so.

General Powell, in the succinct language of a military man, says, "Optimism is a force multiplier." That's perseverance, folks. Optimism is a force multiplier.

You've probably heard of Sandra Day O'Connor, the first woman ever to serve as a Supreme Court Justice. She graduated from the Stanford University Law School in 1952. She graduated near the top of her class and she figured she would get hired immediately by a top law firm. But in 1952 there were very few women attorneys. The only job offers that Sandra Day O'Connor received were for legal secretary positions. But she persevered. She found a new route to victory. She did not even think about giving up.

Instead of joining a top law firm, she started her career as an assistant county attorney. Later, she opened her own law practice with her husband. Twenty nine years after graduating from Stanford — 29 years — Sandra Day O'Connor got a call from the Attorney General of the United States telling her that President Reagan had nominated her to serve on the Supreme Court. My father was honored to do the interview and background check on Sandra Day O'Connor. He performed that role as Chief of Staff to Senator Thurmond, who was serving as Chairman of the Judiciary Committee, which was reviewing Mrs. O'Connor's nomination.

I would like to have seen the expression on the faces of some of the attorneys at the so-called top law firms who had originally turned Sandra Day O'Connor down for a job! But she persevered. She never gave up. She kept working in her chosen profession and she ended up serving on the highest court in our nation. Perseverance.

And do you know what else is interesting? Neither of Sandra Day O'Connor's parents had ever attended college themselves. Her father's family was so poor that he had to work on their farm to help make ends meet. He never got a chance. And college wasn't even an option for Sandra Day O'Connor's mother in those days. But when Sandra was born, her mother began home-schooling her at the age of four. She read to her hour after hour. She persevered. She ended up with a daughter on the Supreme Court!

Our Belief Makes Us Persevere

The scientist, Madame Curie, said, "Life is not easy for any of us. But what of that? We must have perseverance and confidence in ourselves. We must believe that we are gifted for something, and that this thing, at whatever cost, must be attained."

John Lyly Eupheus said, "It is the disposition of the thought that altereth the nature of the thing." It's how you think. When it looks like you can't do it, it's how you think. Because if you think differently you'll find a way to do it.

Henry Ford said, "If you think you can or think you can't, you're right."

A lot of people develop a defeatist attitude as they go through life. They don't always win so they begin to approach assignments expecting to lose. Can you imagine? How can you ever win… how can you ever expect to persevere… if you go into a situation, any situation, expecting to lose. It is the disposition of the thought that altereth the nature of the thing.

I am here to tell you that you can succeed against great odds, you can and will overcome great adversity, if you persevere.

Thomas Edison, the great inventor, was once asked by a reporter, "What have you got to say about the fact that you have failed thousands of times in your attempts to create the light bulb?"

Edison replied. "I beg your pardon. I have never failed even once. I've had thousands of learning experiments that didn't work. I had to run through enough learning experiences to find a way that it did work."

Just think how much further ahead we would be if we could learn to approach our so-called failures as mere learning experiences. In fact, before you succeed, you should expect failure after failure. This is particularly true in science and in research. That's why scientists and inventors like Madame Curie and Thomas Edison are such great models of perseverance. You must have great perseverance to be a great scientist and we can learn a lot from their examples because the same principle of refusing to give up in the face of obstacles applies to our lives.

Whether its starting a business… building a business… running for elective office… working for a good cause at a nonprofit organization, pursuing a career in art or music… and certainly when it comes to raising a family and teaching your children what they need to know to be successful, the same principle of perseverance applies. In my own life, I have used those who are involved in the sciences as an inspiration because they face failure, and must overcome it, literally every single day of their careers. Let me share with you a brief excerpt from a speech about overcoming that the former Chairman of the Polaroid Corporation gave to his employees. Here's what he said, "In the physical sciences, in chemistry and physics and in mathematics when you work in lab, you fail, fail, fail, fail. When you have failed enough times, you ultimately develop 3,000-speed film. If you want color film, you have to fail 10 times as many times. Failure is the very essence of progress.

"The secret is to fail without emotion or embarrassment. A scientist is a person who is a continuous failure. The product of his constant failure is the success that has built our entire world. It is the technique of failure without emotion, the use of failure as a method of learning that has made science.

"But in the social sciences, we start an experiment on how to make you twice the person you are, and we fail the first week and everybody laughs. They say, 'Well, she should have known better,' or 'He didn't have the background' or 'You can't change human nature,' or some other excuse like that.

"The trouble with experimentation in the social sciences is that we are always feeling guilty about failure. We must get used to the idea that we are going to have a thousand failures. We are going to try and fail, try and fail, and look back and to our amazement, find out that each of you has some talents you did not know you had, you learned some things you did not know you could learn, you made some things that you did not know you could make."

Here is how the Chairman of the Polaroid Corporation concluded his speech. Again, he is talking to his employees and what he has to say applies to all of us, "This is the experiment we want to get into. We have no alternative. History is giving you no alternative. It's this or nothing. It's an exciting opportunity. You are lucky. People are always lucky if they have something to do and there is still a chance to do it. You still have that chance... you still have the chance to make history."

That's how I feel. We all have our own chances to make history. In the movie Apollo 13 when they are having significant mechanical failure on the spacecraft, Ed Harris plays the character who is in charge of the Mission Control team. He says, "Failure is not an option." That's how we have to feel. We may face failure... we may actually fail at our first attempt or our second or third or fourth attempt. But ultimately we are going to keep trying until we succeed at carrying out our vision because failure is simply not an option.

I will always remember something Ronald Reagan once said that goes to the heart of perseverance. It stuck in my mind because it rang so true.

One day, Reagan was delivering a speech at a well-known university when he was getting heckled by a student. The student demanded to know how Reagan could ever presume to offer advice to the younger generation. "What do you know about who we are and what we want?" the young heckler yelled. "You're from a different age. When you were born there were no computers, no spacecraft, no superhighways, no space telescopes, no polio vaccine, no organ transplants - there wasn't even television."

"I know," Reagan responded. "You're right, we invented them all."

That's how I look at it. The people who have come before us — and I'm not just talking about famous people, I'm talking about our parents and grandparents and great grandparents — all of them persevered to achieve something. It's the same principle. Now its our turn to do it. And we can do what we set out to do. We can work hard enough and long enough to achieve our dreams in life. I have seen it happen too many times to think anything else. History does not give us any options. Failure is not an option because giving up is not an option.

Most people don't realize this but Oprah Winfrey, who is arguably the most successful person on television today, was a "failure" early in her career. The only thing that saved her career was her perseverance.

Early in her TV career, when she was working in Baltimore, Oprah was taken off the air. She was told that she was no longer good enough for TV and that she could not anchor the news. Her producers didn't like the fact that she empathized with the people she was reporting on. So they demoted her and threw her into the talk show arena. This was back in 1978 before talk shows were popular so Oprah figured that this was it for her, the end of her TV career. Then she realized that she was a better talk show host than a news anchorwoman. And for the past decade, she has had one of the most popular shows ever, and she has made millions of dollars doing it.

Recently, she said, "People need to turn their wounds into wisdom. You will be wounded many times during your life. Some people will call them failures but I have learned that failure is just a way of learning you may be moving in the wrong direction. It's just an experience to learn from. I took what had been a mistake, what had been perceived as a failure with my career as an anchor woman in the news business and turned it into a talk show career. It set me free."

Don't be afraid to fail. The writer, George Bernard Shaw, said, "The man who has never made a mistake will never make anything." It's perseverance.

Aldous Huxley wrote, "Experience is not what happens to the man. It is what a man does with what happens to him."

Turn Your Wounds Into Wisdom

Most people don't know this, but Walt Disney went bankrupt several times and had a nervous breakdown before he finally met with success. Albert Einstein, believe it or not, once failed math. Michael Jordan was cut from his high school's varsity basketball team as a sophomore. Scottie Pippen did even worse in high school — he was the equipment manager before he actually played on the team.

Now all of these people possessed tremendous individual talent. Walt Disney was a visionary. He understood the potential of animation to entertain people. Albert Einstein was a genius despite his initial trouble with math. Michael Jordan and Scottie Pippen clearly had the physical attributes to play basketball. But none of these immensely talented individuals would have succeeded without perseverance. They failed initially, but they kept going. They persevered.

My Country Sent Me To Finish The Race

In college, I was a scholarship football player. I played against opponents who were a lot bigger and stronger and faster than I was. In fact, it was said that I was the smallest down lineman in the nation who was starting for a Division I school. The only reason I made it was because I persevered. I had the will to win. I was the recipient of an Associated Press national award. That was tremendously gratifying because it made a lot of the effort and the pain worthwhile. It taught me at a relatively early age that you can accomplish something if you just stick with it.

I like to study athletes because, for so many of them, perseverance is the key to their success. I think all of us can learn a lot from studying the habits of winning athletes.

Pat McCormick was a diver for the USA in the Helsinki Games of 1952, and the Melbourne Games of 1956. Here's what she said about her work ethic:"The routine never changed, 100 dives per day, six days per week, 12 months per year." Over and over and over — with no adulation... with no glory. Pat McCormick maintained this training regimen just to qualify for the United States Olympic team. But that's what it took.

And so I need to ask you, are you doing what it takes to succeed? Are you persevering? Can you honestly say that you have done everything possible to succeed in your chosen endeavor?

Another example. Billy Mills was a 10,000 meter runner for the United States in the 1964 Olympics hosted by Tokyo.

He was an unknown. Most sports reporters predicted that he would be lucky to finish in the top ten. One reporter asked him what his pre-race strategy would be. Billy Mills said, "To go out with the top four runners and hope for the best."

That's positive, "To hope for the best."

Let me tell you something, as you pursue life, "hope" is a powerful word. Baltazar Gracian says, "Hope is a great falsifier of truth."

The starter of the race sounded the gun and halfway through the race Billy Mills realized he was one second off his best time. And the first thing that entered his mind was this, "I'm not supposed to succeed yet." Here's what he thought: "I'm not supposed to win."

He kept running. And with one lap to go, he moved into first place. But then he dropped down to third. What's amazing is he was sitting in third after experiencing what it could be like to be in first place. Here's what he said to himself, "There's still a chance. There's still a chance. I can win. I can win. I can win."

He accelerated back into second place and then back into first place and as he's thinking, "I can win... I can win... I can win" he broke the tape. First place, gold medal.

Billy Mills was such an underdog, such an unknown, that a Japanese official came up to him after the race and said, "Who are you?" And to this day, Billy Mills is the only American ever to win the 10,000 meter race in the Olympics.

I urge you to learn from the lives of people like Billy Mills... and people like Derek Redman, a 400-meter runner for Great Britain in the Barcelona Games of 1992. He had to withdraw from the 1988 Olympic Games in Seoul because of a pulled Achilles tendon. He was in the semi-finals in Barcelona with seven other men.

His dad, Jim Redman, his biggest fan, was sitting up in the stands watching him compete. This was Derek's last Olympics so he needed to get through the semi-finals and into the finals if he had any chance for a medal. Derek had been plagued by injuries his whole career and this was his final Olympic competition.

This was his moment… his opportunity to do something for himself and for his country. The gun sounded and halfway around the track he heard a pop. He knew immediately that he had pulled a hamstring.

If you watched the Olympics in 1992 then you may have seen Derek Redman stop right in the middle of the track, and the seven other runners passed him in the blink of an eye.

Up in the stands, all his dad could say was, "Oh, no." His dad ran down out of the stands and grabbed his son while the paramedics were running over with a stretcher to take him away, and his son broke down, crying. His dad said, "Come on, son, we have to go." And here's a guy who had every reason to walk away. He said, "I can't go. I have to finish."

This was on international TV. His dad grabbed him and he said, "Well, if you're going to finish, then I'm going to finish with you." He didn't get a gold medal, he didn't get a silver medal, he didn't get a bronze medal, but he claimed a greater medal that day than anybody who broke the tape ahead of him, because he finished… he persevered… he showed the absolute highest resolve.

Let's look at the marathon in Mexico City in 1968. Abebe Bikila for Ethiopia was striving toward his third gold medal. After the gun sounded he stopped because of a stress fracture in his left leg. One of his countrymen saw him and picked up the mantle for Ethiopia and ran the rest of the way, winning the gold medal. That's not the story, although it's a great story and was on the front page of all the newspapers.

But there was a better story. A full hour after the Ethiopian had won the race, another runner entered the stadium for the final lap round the track. Most people had either already gone home or were making their way to the exits.

The runner was bloodied and bandaged. A reporter looked up from the story he was writing and said, "It's the last man in the marathon." The runner's name was John Stephen Akhwari from Tanzania.

And it was just like a Rocky movie. You know when you're sitting there in the movie theater and all of a sudden the applause starts real slow and then builds to a great ovation? Well, it happens in real life too.

The spectators that night in the Olympic stadium in Mexico City started to notice this last runner, John Stephen Akhwari. People began to realize what was happening as they put their hands together. The applause grew louder and louder as Akhwari moved around the track and picked up the pace. He started running faster and faster and faster to finish. There was no gold medal for him... there was no silver or bronze medal for him. But he crossed the finish line.

The lead story the next day read, "Today we have seen a young African runner who symbolizes the finest in the human spirit, a performance that gives meaning to the word courage. All honor to John Stephen Akhwari from Tanzania."

The reporters asked him, "Why'd you even take the time to finish? You could have stopped, no one would have ever known." He looked at the reporter and here's all he said, "I don't think you understand. My country did not send me to Mexico to start the race. My country sent me to finish the race."

Success Is Right Around The Corner

In the Kimberly Diamond fields of South Africa, they sift through approximately 86 tons of dirt in order to discover one carat of diamonds. That's perseverance toward a goal. And that's what we need to do in our own lives. We need to be able to see the diamonds... to recognize the rewards that are waiting for us if we are willing to dig deeply enough within our own souls.

Never give up. You can do anything you want if you stick to it long enough. Keep your thoughts and your mind always on the goal. Franklin Roosevelt said, "When you come to the end of your rope, tie a knot and hang on."

The famous author, William Blake, one wrote, "Great things are done when men and mountains meet." Now, obviously, if Mr. Blake were writing today he would have said "when men and women and mountains meet." But I really like this imagery of mountains as challenge and struggle. We are all climbing some personal mountain of our own. If we're not, then we should be.

When the first two people conquered Mount Everest, Sir Edmund Hillary and his sherpa guide Tenzing, they achieved greatness. They did not achieve greatness by taking an easy stroll down the garden path. They achieved greatness because everyone recognized that it was through a tremendous struggle that they were able to place their feet on top of the world's highest mountain. It was something no one else had ever done before. In that was their greatness. They persevered.

Keep climbing. Don't stop. So many people give up when success is right around the corner. If you are willing to persevere, you can accomplish so much with your life. And you should draw inspiration from all of the men and women who have come before you who overcame so much to be successful — so much more than most of us have to face.

I mentioned Albert Einstein earlier. He did not speak until he was four years old and he did not learn to read until he was seven. One of his teachers described him as "mentally slow, unsociable, and forever adrift in his dreams."

Henry Ford failed and went broke five times before he finally succeeded. Babe Ruth may have hit 714 home runs but he had to strike out more than 1300 times to do it. After the great actor and dancer Fred Astaire's first screen test, the memo from the testing director of MGM studio, dated 1933, said, "He can't act. Slightly bald. Can dance a little." Fred Astaire kept that memo above his fireplace at home in Beverly Hills as an inspiration. Maybe you have received some rejection letters over the years that you should keep around and frame after you have made it big.

Hang on to your dreams. Don't let them slip away. Keep going. So many people give up when they're just one step, one call, one day from achieving their vision. Don't quit. Don't be one of the people who stop just before they make it. Keep your mind always focused on your goals. Finish what you start.

Always work. If you fail, stand up. "We fight, get beat, rise and fight again." "Let only Americans stand watch this night." Be worthy of your heritage by never giving up. Be responsible for your failures. When I talk to great people about their successes some say, "You just see me in the spotlight, you've never seen me in my moments of failure. This is all you see but I failed many times to get here." So be responsible for your failures as well as your successes. When other people have quit and you're alone, use those quiet moments to keep yourself going. If you think you can do it, you will. Nothing in the world can take the place of perseverance.

The writer Samuel Johnson wrote, "Great works are not performed with strength, but by perseverance."

No matter what happens, don't give up. Set your course and stay with it. Keep going and sooner or later you will reach your goals. You can do it. Perseverance will enable you to win. Live to win!

CHAPTER FOUR
RESPONSIBILITY

"There is a price tag on human liberty. That price is the willingness to assume the responsibilites of being free men." – *Eugene Holman*

I previously discussed the necessity of having a vision of greatness for your life. Additionally, we examined how courage and perseverance are necessary ingredients to help you achieve your vision. In this chapter, I'll explore why accepting responsibility is absolutely essential in living to win.

When it comes to describing the importance of responsibility, I think Winston Churchill summed it up best. He said, "The price of greatness is responsibility."

It's that simple. Greatness is yours. It's there. It's within your reach. But you will never attain any lasting success unless you first decide to accept responsibility.

We all need to assume responsibility for our successes and our failures. If we are not willing to shoulder the lessons of our own defeats, then we will never enjoy the euphoria of triumph. Stand tall, measure up, and claim the losses as well as the victories.

Every successful individual — entrepreneurs, business owners, athletes, musicians, artists, teachers and elected leaders will tell you winning means paying the price. And the price of greatness is responsibility.

As I travel around the world and speak to different groups, I oftentimes remind the adults in the audience of something they already know: "We are all just kids in grown-up bodies." When my wife, Sandy, and I became parents, she jokingly said, "Well, I guess now we have to be responsible." Up until then the only babies we had were dogs. I'm sure you have had similar moments in your life when you said to yourself, to a loved one, or to a colleague, "Well, this is it. Time to accept responsibility."

That's a transforming moment, to accept responsibility. To own responsibility. The Walt Disney movie *The Lion King* is a great movie on several different levels, but what it's really about is accepting responsibility.

I won't ruin it for you if you haven't seen it, but the Lion King, Simba, gets separated from his family when he's just a cub. He ends up living with a big, fat Warthog and a little meerkat. All they do all day long is goof around and eat bugs. They call their lifestyle *Hakuna Matata* - it's their equivalent of "Don't worry, be happy." One of the other lions discovers where Simba is living, and forces him to choose between a life of Hakuna Matata or to accept his rightful place of responsibility and leadership as the King. There are great lessons in this movie.

I know what a challenge it can be to take responsibility — we've all been there. But true, lasting success is not going to just fall into your lap. It's not going to search you out. Lasting, life-fulfilling success is not an accident, it's not like winning the lottery.

Real success requires that we take control of our destiny, that we stop letting life be something that just happens.

John D. Rockefeller, the great American industrialist, said, "I believe that every right implies a responsibility; every opportunity an obligation; every possession a duty."

Look for a moment at the word "responsibility." It combines "response" and "ability." We each have the freedom to choose our response.

Proactive people recognize and accept their responsibilities. Truly accepting responsibility is like becoming a parent. Any healthy man can father a baby, any healthy woman can give birth. But having children means only that the work of becoming a parent has begun. The biological event is very different from the actual responsibility of being a parent — the love and commitment... the skinned knees and the dirty diapers... the faithfulness to homework and Little League... the sacrifices for music lessons and college tuition... the laughter and the tears. Accepting these responsibilities, ideally with love and grace, add up to earning the title, "mom" and "dad."

It's assuming responsibility for your successes as well as your failures. As I mentioned earlier, I grew up in Virginia right across the Potomac River from the Washington Monument. My father is Senator Strom Thurmond's Chief of Staff. One day, my dad and I were walking with the Senator. He's 96-years-old. We were walking over to the 16th annual National Peace Officers Memorial Service in Washington, DC, right in front of the Capitol building

I asked Senator Thurmond a very simple question. I said, "Why is it some people succeed and other people fail with exactly the same opportunity?" He looked at me and didn't bat an eye. He said, "Because they don't accept responsibility." It was simple. It was very simple and very eloquent. You have got to be responsible.

Responsibility Empowers You

America's first seven astronauts were put through an incredible battery of tests as they prepared for their first mission into the final frontier. Some of the toughest tests were simulations of the launch and then re-entry into the Earth's orbit. The astronauts were exposed to extremes in temperature, turbulence, g-forces, and other stresses that most of us would not want to experience.

The mission control staff conducted an important experiment involving responsibility. They constructed two simulators. In one, the astronauts were simply buckled into their seats and had no control over their surroundings. They were along for the ride, so to speak. In the other simulator, there was a switch, a simple toggle switch. If the stresses became too much to handle, the astronaut had the option of reaching out and switching off the simulator.

No astronaut ever even reached for the switch, let alone used it. But as the mission control staff monitored the simulations, they learned something really interesting about human nature. And it applies to us. When they were in the simulator with the switch, the astronauts displayed lower blood pressures, lower body temperatures, and slower heart rates.

In other words, they were able to cope more effectively with the extreme stresses and pressures when they were given responsibility for controlling the test. The ability to accept responsibility over their surroundings actually relaxed the astronauts, they were empowered by it.

We're the same way. Taking responsibility strengthens us. Obviously, life does not come with an on/off switch; we don't have the option of saying, "Stop the world, I want to get off!" But taking responsibility for who we are and what we do is a heck of a lot better than just being along for the ride. If we accept responsibility, then we help control our journey. The alternative is just to sit back and let life pass us by. If that happens, I guarantee that you will end up somewhere you don't want to be.

The need to take control, or responsibility, in business is the same way. I hear people talk about so-called "small business owners." Well, your business may seem small to people on the outside but if you own it, it's pretty darn big. Do you know what I mean? Owning a business, being responsible for the people you employ, building it so you have enough income to support your family are big responsibilities. I don't care how large or small your business is. Take responsibility for your business and you feel it night and day.

And besides, I don't think anybody sets out and says, "I'm going to start and build a small business." No, you begin a business and nurture it. You take responsibility for its growth, it doesn't just happen. Bill Gates didn't wake up one day and say, "I'm going to start a small computer company." He birthed an infant company, he accepted responsibility for its health and well-being, and helped grow it into a mature enterprise. For that matter, he and his people are still growing Microsoft.

Let me give you another example about accepting responsibility. Maybe you know the story about Aaron Feuerstein, the president and CEO of a textile company called Malden Mills. The company has 3,000 employees; it is the largest employer in the town of Lawrence, Massachusetts. The story about Feuerstein and his company made headlines a few years ago.

On the night of Feuerstein's 70th birthday, he was at a surprise birthday party and, boy, did he get quite a surprise. Most of his company's manufacturing buildings burned to the ground that night. All of a sudden the future of those 3,000 employees was in Feuerstein's hands.

That night, the same night as the fire, Feuerstein held a press conference and announced that he would rebuild Malden Mills. He announced that he would continue to pay all of his employees for 90 days until they could re-open the plant… and he would continue to pay their medical benefits.

This was at a time when a lot of textile companies were either moving south or moving overseas so that the owners could make more money. When Feuerstein was asked why he didn't use the fire as an excuse to pick up and move his company, here's what he said: "While I watched the fire I didn't cry because it was no time to feel sorry for myself. I knew I had a very big responsibility being the chief officer, and that I had to rebuild. I was determined to rebuild. By rebuilding we would be able to save the jobs of 3,000 people. We could save the town. That was my obligation. It would have been unthinkable to make a deal with the insurance company and just take the cash. A lot of people suggested that, but it would have left 3,000 people without work and it would have bankrupted the city of Lawrence."

Today, Malden Mills is operating at full strength; in fact, it has expanded since the fire. Now that's responsibility.

I met another CEO recently named Russ Reid. He shared a similar story about accepting responsibility during a tough time in the life of a business. Back in the '60s, Russ founded a marketing and communications company in Chicago to help nonprofit organizations raise money. The Russ Reid Company enjoyed some early success, but then Russ made a couple of business decisions that didn't work out.

One Friday afternoon, he realized he was going to have trouble making payroll. Here's what Russ told me: "I sat there at my desk and said, 'You know, if things were going well and we were making a fortune, I would take credit for that. But we were failing. And I had to take credit for that, too.'"

Russ kept working, he sold off some of the investments he had made that weren't working, and today the Russ Reid Company is the largest marketing and communications firm in the nation that specializes in serving nonprofit organizations.

I had an interesting experience in my own life, recently, that reminded me of the importance of accepting responsibility. I visited my old high school. I stood next to my old locker and when I looked up I saw my reflection in the window, I saw a man who is 40 years old. And this is what hit me: I have made a lot of great decisions in my life. And I have made a lot of bad decisions.

But here's the point — I've made decisions. Sometimes they were right and sometimes they were wrong. But I made the decisions and I accepted the responsibility for them.

Most people go through life and don't make decisions. They keep putting them off. It always seems a lot easier to put off decisions, so people put them off, and then they die. They die, and then of course it's too late to make decisions.

Accepting responsibility when things go wrong is extremely important as well. Ronald Reagan had a sign on his desk in the Oval Office that said, "You can accomplish a lot if you don't care who gets the credit." So here's my advice to you when you're working with other people. If something goes right, give your team the credit. if something goes wrong, you accept the responsibility for it. People will respect you for doing it.

Rights Come With Responsibilities

I'm always struck by the fact that, here in America, most people really like to talk about our rights. People write about them in editorials, you see people arguing about rights on TV talk shows, you hear people talking about rights on the radio. Growing up in Washington, I saw numerous protests where people came from all over the country to march for their rights. While we are blessed to live in a nation that gives us this freedom, it is imperative that we understand that each one of our rights are entwined with responsibilities.

As you read the Declaration of Independence, the beginning establishes those rights of life, liberty and the pursuit of happiness. But do you know what's really interesting? Read the last line of the Declaration of Independence.

It's the most eloquent line in the document. It says, "We mutually pledge our lives, our fortunes, and our sacred honor." Let me repeat, "Our sacred honor." That's responsibility. We can't have one without the other. With all of our rights come responsibilities. Just as we have a fair claim on our rights, America's sacred honor — our sacred honor — has a claim on us. The 56 men who signed the Declaration of Independence, and other leaders of the American Revolutionary War, would either become glorious Founders of a new nation or they would swing from a hanging tree. As Benjamin Rush said, his fellow signers knew they were signing their own "death warrants."

Nathan Hale did not sign the Declaration of Independence. He was a school teacher. But he willingly upheld his sacred honor with his own life. Nathan Hale volunteered to join the Continental Army during the Revolution. After being commissioned as a First Lieutenant he was assigned to recruit new soldiers up and down the coast of Connecticut.

Time and time again Nathan proved his value to this new army of rag-tag soldiers and was promoted to Captain. However, at the time, the war was not going very well for the colonists, especially at the harbor of New York City. General Washington asked for a group of the most outstanding soldiers known to be assembled, out of which one would volunteer to complete a very special task. The volunteer was to go behind enemy lines, learn the plans of the British, draw maps of their fortifications, write notes in code, and return with the information.

Nathan volunteered the very next morning, and, dressed as a schoolteacher, began his secret mission. He easily made his way through the enemy lines to Long Island. He was successful in writing notes and drawing maps, which he hid in his shoe. After about a week, Nathan was captured after listening in on a meeting where plans were being discussed on how to capture Washington's army on Manhattan Island.

Nathan Hale was searched. The notes were found in his shoe and he was sentenced to be hanged the following morning. The next day, while waiting for his execution, he was asked if there was anything he would like to have. He asked for a Bible. There was not one available so he asked for paper and a pen instead. He began with the heading "New York City, September 22, 1776," and he poured his thoughts out on paper as he wrote two letters to his family. He was promised by an English Captain that they would be delivered to his brother Enoch.

Slowly, but calmly, Nathan walked to the cart that had been placed under a tree. A rope was hanging from one of the limbs. From the cart, Nathan looked over the small crowd that had gathered. Some of the faces looked scornful. Many showed pity. "Don't you know that you're about to die?"an English officer asked him. "Yes, I know," Nathan said quietly. The officer said, "I have never seen anyone like you! Don't you have any regrets?"

Nathan Hale looked at the people without fear and spoke in an unwavering voice. "I only regret that I have but one life to lose for my Country!" It's an incredibly powerful story.

The responsibility of the freedoms we now enjoy needs to motivate and push us toward attaining more knowledge... greater accomplishments... new innovations and technological developments... and more prosperity.

We should be proud and thankful for the opportunity to protect our rights with our sacred honor. Our sense of responsibility should be every bit as clear and as automatic as our sense of rights. I love the story of Sergeant Stephen Trujillo for that very reason.

Sergeant Trujillo was a medic in the 2nd Ranger Battalion, 75th Infantry, during our liberation of Grenada in 1983. He was in the first helicopter to land at the compound held by Cuban forces in Grenada. As his helicopter landed, he saw three others crash. Despite the imminent explosion of the burning aircraft, he never hesitated. He ran across 25 yards of open terrain through enemy fire to rescue wounded soldiers. He directed two other medics, administered first aid, and returned again and again to the crash site to carry his wounded friends to safety.

That day in Grenada, Sergeant Trujillo and his fellow service men and women not only saved innocent lives, they helped set a nation free. I know it must have taken great courage to do what they did. What strikes me about Sergeant Trujillo is the responsibility of his heroic actions. He did not hesitate, he obviously did not think of himself first. He had a job to do. He had a duty, an obligation. And he did it without flinching.

Mission accomplished. He accepted responsibility. I know it can seem tough sometimes... but it's our sacred honor.

We should be proud of our heritage, and we should honor our heritage by being responsible citizens. The best way to honor the giants of our history is to go forward and accept responsibility for continuing what they began.

Did you know that the United States is one of the youngest nations on earth but our Constitution is one of the oldest? We have used the same Constitution to govern our country longer than almost any other nation on earth. When we study other nations we see how often they change their form of government... they overthrow their leaders and write completely new constitutions.

The United States of America's Constitution is special, it's unique. It comes down to responsibility. I love world history so I have read the constitutions of several different countries. I read the constitution of the Soviet Union before that nation collapsed. In fact, a lot of people I talk to are surprised when I tell them that the Soviet Union even had a constitution. But it did.

The Soviet Constitution even granted a number of freedoms to its people. Many countries have written into their constitutions different provisions that supposedly give their people the freedom of speech and the freedom of assembly, among others.

"We The People..."

Do you know what makes the Constitution of the United States so exceptional? The difference is so small that it's easy to miss. But the difference is so great that it tells you the whole story in just three words. Those three words are, "We the people." It's responsibility, folks.

In those other constitutions, the government tells the people of those countries what they are allowed to do. In our constitution, "we the people" tell the government what it is allowed to do. Virtually every other revolution in history just exchanged one set of rulers for another set of rulers. But the American Revolution created a new government - our democracy has been called "The Great Experiment" - where the people are the masters. Responsibility. We can't get away from it. It's there.

Abraham Lincoln said, "You can't escape the responsibility of tomorrow by evading it today."

We the people — are the young men and women who fought in Operation Desert Storm, the Gulf War. They're the ones who kept Saddam Hussein out of Kuwait so that he couldn't control the world's oil supply.

We the people — are the parents who take responsibility for teaching their children the values that will last them a lifetime... like duty and honor, commitment and respect. It's the parents who sacrifice long and hard so their children can attend the college they never got to go to... so that their children will know a better life.

We the people — are the entrepreneurs who are risking something to pursue a vision and create jobs with dignity in the private sector. It's the businessmen and women who get to work an hour early, who stay an hour late, who demonstrate their leadership by actually serving the people who work for them. It's responsibility.

We the people — are the people who volunteer to help whenever is a hurricane or a flood or a tornado... those are the people who feed, clothe, and teach the needy so that they, too, can become productive citizens.

We the people —it's us. It's you and me. It's up to us to be responsible enough to preserve and protect the rights that have been bestowed upon us.

The most exciting revolution ever known to humankind began with those three simple words - "We the People." We created the revolutionary notion that the people grant government its rights, and not the other way around. There's one lesson that has come home powerfully to me, which I would offer to you. Just as those leaders who created the United States of America pledged to each other their lives, their fortunes and their sacred honor, so too we must pledge to each other that we will keep foremost in our hearts and minds not what is best for ourselves, but what is best for each other. Our husbands and wives and children, our business partners and employees, our friends and neighbors. We have a responsibility to them that we need to accept and fulfill.

We can do it. It's a lot easier for us than it was for the Founding Fathers. No one is threatening our lives. No one is threatening our livelihoods. We simply need to accept our responsibilities and motivate ourselves to fulfill them. Don't ever go backward. Go forward. Keep the sun rising in your own life. Give your best by accepting responsibilities for both your victories and your defeats. If you do that, I guarantee you, you will have many more victories. You will be living to win.

Being Responsible For Who You Become

One thing I say everywhere I go is that you are nothing more than a sum total of the books you have read in your life, the people you take advice from, and the people you hang out with. It's our responsibility to make sure we're reading the right books. It's our responsibility to listen to the right people for advice. And it's our responsibility to hang out with the right people. Thomas Bailey Aldridge said, "A man is known by the company his mind keeps."

So I encourage you to read books. Read biographies and autobiographies of great people who accomplished great things in their lives. Descartes said in the *Discourse on Method*, "The reading of all good books is like conversation with the finest men of past centuries."

You can tell everything about a person based on what they read.

John Adams was an avid reader and life-long learner. John Adams' father was a farmer and a shoemaker but Adams was educated as a lawyer. As a young man, he promised himself never to allow "one hour to pass unimproved... I will rouse up my mind and fix my attention. I will stand collected within myself and think upon what I read and what I see." Responsibility.

Teddy Roosevelt's home was a place of habitual learning and constant reinforcement. His father always encouraged him to seize the moment. Abraham Lincoln, as a young man, was rarely without a book in his hand. Harry Truman's parents admonished him to be good, work hard on the family farm, and told him he could be anything he wanted to be. Later in life, Truman recalled never being bored because "we had a house full of books."

Benjamin Franklin, Thomas Jefferson, James Madison, and John Adams were all continual learners who surrounded themselves with books of all kinds. So read good books.

And take advice from the right people.

Wilma Rudolph once said, "My doctors told me I would never walk again. My mother told me I would. I believed my mother." It made all the difference in Wilma Rudolph's life who she took her advice from.

Perhaps you recognize her name. As a child, Wilma Rudolph had double pneumonia and scarlet fever. These two diseases combined to paralyze her left leg. She had to wear an iron leg brace.

But Wilma Rudolph was blessed to have a mother who took her responsibility as a parent seriously. She encouraged her daughter, she nurtured her. At age nine, the leg brace came off. By age 12, Wilma had taught herself to run. At age 13, she entered a race — and she came in last, by the way. She finished dead last. In the next race, she finished next to last. She kept moving up. Finally, she won a race in high school.

Wilma went to college and joined the track team. Her coach began training her. In 1960, she was good enough to qualify for the Olympics. In the 100 meters, she faced a German woman who had never been beaten, but Wilma won. In the 200 meters, Wilma Rudolph won again. And in the 400-meter relay, Wilma Rudolph came from behind running the anchor leg and won her third Olympic gold medal.

Wilma Rudolph made history that day because she became the first woman ever to win three gold medals at the same

Olympics. I'd say it mattered who Wilma Rudolph took her advice from. And it matters just as much in your own life. Take advice from the right people.

I tell people all the time, "If you want to become successful in any endeavor, hang around people who are successful in that area." You have a choice. You can hang around with people who made it or the people who didn't make it. If you're not hanging around the right people, then you never have the opportunity to get advice from the right people... the people who've made it. If you want a successful marriage, hang around people with successful marriages. And ask questions. Ask lots of questions. "How did you get through this? How did you do it? What kept you going? How can I be successful?"

I think another way to understand the importance of choosing who you hang around with is to look at people coming out of prison. They mark down the days until they are scheduled to be released. They don't dream of ever going back into prison. They don't write on their calendar, "I want to come back on January 1st." They're marking down the days with big red Xs because they want to get out.

But what happens? They finally get out of prison and they go back into the same neighborhoods where they were before going to prison. They begin to hang out with the same people they got into trouble with in the first place. Then, because of their association, they get into trouble again.

So be careful who you associate with. Sometimes we all need to change who we associate with because those people may be holding us back. We've all been there.

Cervantes says, "Tell me the company and I'll tell thee what thou art." Euripides says, "Every man is known by the company he is wont to keep."

I have a favorite Spanish proverb that says, "It is better to weep with wise men than to laugh with fools." Don't forget it. When you want to accomplish something in your life, when you want to do something great in your life, there will be people who will laugh at you. Remember, "I would rather weep with wise men than to laugh with fools," any day of my life.

George Washington made a very powerful statement. He said, "Where are our men of abilities? Why do they not come forth to save their country?" He also said, "There is an insoluble union between virtue and happiness, between duty and advantage."

The Responsibility Of Service

Responsibility. Let me tell you, one thing that was ingrained in me as a kid, one thing my dad talked about my whole life was servant leadership. And he didn't say you have to run for office to serve. I think everybody should serve.

George Washington taught us a lot about servant leadership. Washington was living a comfortable life in Mount Vernon; he had a beautiful farm there and a relatively easy, peaceful life. But he felt summoned by his country, he felt a sense of duty. And he did not see it as his responsibility to rule over people, but to serve his fellow countrymen. It was the most noble of impulses. And what does that teach us about how we should be living our lives today? It means that a complete life, whether in the 18th century, or in the 21st, must involve service to other people. It's responsibility.

My parents always told me that being an American brings

so many privileges, but each and every one of them is wrapped in responsibility. You can't have one without the other. In the chapter on courage, I discussed Jackie Joyner-Kersee, who overcame violence and illness and being brought up in the ghetto to become the world's greatest female athlete. She has shown her courage before millions of sports fans during the past 15 years.

But in quieter ways she has shown responsibility. She has given a scholarship to a National Merit Scholar from her old high school… she has sent teams of children from her old neighborhood to the AAU Junior Olympic Championships… she has taken 100 children from her hometown to the Thanksgiving Day parade in New York City. She and her husband built a Youth Center in East St. Louis, where she was born.

Why did she do this? It's responsibility.

Most people are familiar with Mark McGwire, the St. Louis Cardinal slugger who broke Roger Maris' supposedly unbreakable record of 61 home runs in a single season. Most people don't know that McGwire considered quitting baseball after a dismal season in 1991 when he hit only 22 home runs and batted an anemic .201.

But he reconsidered when he thought about his younger brother, Jay, who was actually a better baseball prospect but lost an eye in a freak accident that ended his career. He thought about his father, who had been afflicted with polio as a child.

McGwire said, "I was at a crossroads in my career. I remember driving home after the 1991 season. I was so down. I got to thinking about everything my father had been through. I thought about Jay, too, how he had it taken away from him. I thought about how much I really loved the game, and I just decided that there wasn't any room for pouting or complaining or doing anything but my best."

With a renewed understanding of his responsibility to do his best, McGwire also brought a renewed focus to his home run quest. He turned down endorsement offers. He turned down interviews with Jay Leno, David Letterman, and *60 Minutes*. He turned down any offers that seemed to be distractions from the responsibility he felt to be his best in his chosen profession.

And the result? McGwire became the first player in 37 years to break the single-season home run record. Did you watch TV toward the end of the season as he went from game to game and stadium to stadium? All of the fans stood and cheered for him. They embraced his achievements, even the opposing fans, because they sensed his responsibility and commitment to accomplishing something great.

Responsibility Takes Initiative

There are many fine stories of assuming personal responsibility in our every day lives.

As you're driving around, you may have seen cars with a little sign that says, "Baby on Board." If you have children, maybe you have bought one and its hanging in your car now. Well, that little sign was developed by a hair stylist who felt that she and her baby were unsafe when they were in an automobile. She felt that if other drivers knew she had a "baby on board," they might take extra precautions.

She put it in her rear window and, to her amazement, it worked. This woman figured that if it worked for her, it would work for others. So she sold the idea to JC Penney, and she's now making a fortune in royalties.

Most of us know that Jonas Salk is the scientist who developed the vaccine for polio. What has gone largely unnoticed, however, was his motivation to do it in the first place. The story goes that Salk was a 30-year-old medical researcher when his mother said to him, "Jonas, your brother is dying of polio. Why don't you find a cure for it?"

Salk replied, "Mom, I never took it as my own commitment or responsibility. But I love my brother more than myself, so I will do it." He proceeded to work around the clock until he came up with the Salk Vaccine.

During a recession, Delta Airlines doubled the number of planes it owned. The leaders at Delta told their employees, "We are going to keep all of you working." The employees were so thankful they actually helped Delta pay for the planes.

You may recall the newspaper stories about John Tu and David Sun, the two young founders of Kingston Technology Corporation. Kingston is the world's leading manufacturer of memory upgrades for computers. They sold 80 percent of the company to a Japanese computer publishing giant in 1996 for $1.5 billion. The two founders didn't simply take the money and run. They felt a responsibility to the people who had helped make them so successful - their employees. So they set aside $100 million from their own pockets to give away as bonuses. So far they have paid out $40 million of it, averaging $76,000 per employee.

Take the billionaire investor George Soros. Born in Hungary, Soros feels tremendously responsible for helping the former Soviet Union go from being the ultimate communist state to capitalism now that the Cold War is over. Soros has poured $260 million into Russia since 1994 and he has pledged another $500 million to help establish everything from business training programs to hospitals to prisons. Why? Because he believes it's the responsible thing to do.

Now, most of us are not billionaires — but what's important is not just the gift but the sense of duty and responsibility behind the gift.

We need to share our talents and the successes we've had with other people who are less fortunate than we are. That's part of what it means to be responsible. Franklin Delano Roosevelt once said, "The test of our progress is not whether we add more to the abundance of those who have much. It is whether we provide enough to those who have little."

You know, we are living at a time when most people are skeptical about politics and politicians. I totally understand that. In fact, I believe that healthy skepticism is a good thing. Our young people need a healthy sense of skepticism to function in the real world. Skepticism challenges the status quo, and I know that too many of our elected officials seem content with the status quo sometimes. Or even worse, they may like to see things change but only in ways that help them or some special interest that they're supporting.

But I do want to say this: I lived in Washington, DC; I grew up there and I guarantee you there are some good folks working there - both the elected officials and their staffs. My father is one of them. There are thousands of folks working on Capitol Hill and the federal agencies who show up every day with a purpose. They're not just pushing paper and collecting a paycheck. Some of them are, sure. But the good ones are keeping the engines of our democracy well oiled. They're the ones who are answering our mail and helping us get White House tours when we visit from home. They're the ones who are making the honest policy decisions that help the people who deserve to be helped.

I admire the men and women who run for elected office.

It's amazing to me what some of them are willing to go through to have the opportunity to serve us. We always hear about the bad ones, but the good ones go to Washington because they want to serve, they feel it's their calling, their duty to serve. They are willing to absorb all the slings and arrows that the media may fire at them so that they can pursue a career in public service.

Some of these good folks leave their businesses, their families, and go serve each and every one of us. We need to lift them up and support them because they are fulfilling their scared honor. I'll guarantee you that if you go to your state capital, if you go into Washington, DC, there are men and women hard at work, serving your state and your country every single day. They could make a lot more money doing other things, but they're not doing it for that, they're doing it for us.

I was at a business meeting recently and somebody said, "Well, listen, one person really doesn't make a difference in the electoral process." I couldn't disagree more. One person makes a boatload of difference in the electoral process because one person influences another person and that person influences another person. That's how things are changed. That's why it always hurts when I see so few people exercising their right, their responsibility, to vote.

In the upcoming congressional elections, it's been predicted that only 34 or 35 percent of the people will get out and vote. We should be ashamed of that. Maybe it's just me, maybe I'm just old fashioned. But our ancestors put their lives on the line for us, gave their lives willingly, and we can't get in our cars and stop by the voting booth on our way to work? Two out of three people are so laissez-faire about our democracy that they don't even bother to vote? I always like to vote, I feel better after I do it. In a way, it's like going to church. Don't you always feel better when you've listened to a good sermon, you sing a few hymns, you shake the hands of some friends, talk to them, and then the doors swing open and you're out in the sunshine? You feel renewed. That's how I feel when I vote. I love it. I wear the sticker that they give you around all day.

We have a responsibility to vote. We have a responsibility to serve. It's our sacred honor.

I also believe we should all serve in some way, even a small way. I encourage you to go serve in the PTA, go serve in your church or synagogue. Become active. Become active in your community. Volunteer to mentor a young boy or girl who doesn't have a dad living at home. Build a house, pound some nails, on a Saturday with a Habitat for Humanity work crew. Put your family in the car and deliver meals to older people who are too frail to leave their homes.

I submit to you that some of your greatest satisfactions in life, some of your best moments, your most memorable times, those times that later make you turn to your spouse or your kids and say, "Remember when we did that?" — they will occur when you are serving others. It's amazing. There was a study done by the Rand Corporation and UCLA on the effects of what they call "service learning" in 500 colleges and universities. Service learning refers to students who participate in some form of community service.

The study found that the students involved in community service had better grades, better life skills, such as leadership ability, and a greater sense of civic responsibility than students who did not participate in any kind of service. The community leaders were surveyed as well. They had nothing but rave reviews for the students. It was truly a win-win situation; it was good for everybody. The moral of the story is simple and obvious — give and you shall receive. That's a good lesson to be learned early and continued through our lives. It's a good lesson to teach our children.

You may be familiar with the term Tzedakah. It is the Hebrew word for the acts that are called *charity* in English. However, the nature of Tzedakah is a little different than charity. The root form of Tzedakah is a word meaning righteousness, justice or fairness.

In Judaism, giving to the poor is not viewed as a generous or magnanimous act. Rather, it is simply an act of justice or responsibility. Certain types of Tzedakah are considered more meritorious than others. There are eight levels of giving. The least meritorious form of Tzedakah is to give grudgingly. The ultimate level is defined as enabling the recipient to become self-reliant. Just think of all the opportunities we have in our businesses and in our communities to make people more self-reliant. It's really just a matter of taking the time, of accepting the responsibility to do it.

If you are a leader, if you are living to win, then you have an opportunity... you have a responsibility... to serve others. It's our sacred honor.

We Americans live in a nation that is now the only superpower on earth, with opportunities for true national greatness. Let's think a moment about the true measurements of greatness. We are obviously the strongest military power in the world. We have the greatest political influence. Economically, we are probably stronger than any other nation. We enjoy a tremendous amount of basic rights.

So the question is, are we measuring up as a nation, which means, are we measuring up as individuals, to our responsibilities? A chain is only as strong as its weakest link. Are you contributing to the strength of our nation? You must. A strong nation rests on the rock of responsibility. Our sacred honor.

We are, each of us, beneficiaries of those who came before us — and not just those who served in the armed forces in times of war. They paid the highest price. Their mark stands forever. But we are all indebted for our institutions, our laws, our music, our paintings, our way of life to those who went before us. This nation didn't just happen. The outcomes of the Revolutionary War and the Civil War, and World War I and World War II, were not pre-ordained. They didn't have to end the way they did.

But people stepped up. They measured up. They took responsibility for the life of our nation and the rest of the free world. As Winston Churchill said, "We haven't come this far because we are made of sugar candy." And remember what else Churchill said, "The price of greatness is responsibility."

One of the lessons of history is that we must appreciate what we have and accept responsibility for maintaining what we have... improving and perfecting it. I believe you have the opportunity to achieve greatness in your life. I know you can do it. I know you will achieve greatness by making decisions, accepting them, and moving forward. Make the tough decisions. By God, don't let your life go by without making the decisions that will ultimately decide what your quality of life is. You are too important for that, your family is too important.

You should be proud of your rights. You should enjoy them, defend them, make the most of them. Accept responsibility for them. Read great books. Study great people. Be selective about who you associate with and take advice from. You will be known by the company you keep. And remember the proverb — it is better to weep with wise men than to laugh with fools. It's "we the people." It's our sacred honor. It's responsibility.

CHAPTER FIVE
CHARACTER

"No man can climb out beyond the limitations of his own character." —John Morely

Character is one of the most difficult words in the English language to define, but it is one of the easiest to describe. The character of a person is something that we can sense almost immediately... and the character of a person is clearly demonstrated over time.

Character is the collection of personal attributes that encompass all of the admirable, inner qualities of human nature. The quality of our character determines the quality of our actions and our leadership; good character is essential to have if you want to live to win.

I think most people are in general agreement about what constitutes good character. It includes such qualities as honesty, self-discipline, fairness, respect for law, duty, decency, tolerance and courage. It was Socrates who said, "The unexamined life is not worth living." Socrates was talking, at least in part, about character. We need to look within ourselves to make sure that we have the right qualities to succeed... to live to win. We need to examine our character. We need to put it under a microscope. Don't be afraid. We all make mistakes, we all do things that are wrong. The point is not to be perfect. What we need to do is understand what makes up good character and then look for opportunities to practice it.

A friend related a story to me about a third grade school teacher he knows. He likes to teach his kids how to juggle. He says that whenever he starts to teach a classroom full of kids how to juggle, a couple of them always raise their hands and say they already know how to do it. So he calls them up to the front of the room and, of course, you know what happens. The same thing that happens to us if we don't know how to juggle. The kids throw the balls in the air and wave their arms around but they don't really know how to juggle. They try to imitate the real thing, but they can't.

Juggling is not something you can fake. Either you can juggle or you can't. One of the reasons juggling has always appealed to this teacher is that juggling is so unambiguous. There are no phony jugglers. If the balls stay in the air, then you can clearly juggle. The ability to juggle is always genuine. You have to learn to be able to do it. Character is exactly the same way. A person's character, whether it's good or bad, is always genuine. It has to be learned. And you might try to fake good character, but sooner or later, it becomes obvious who you really are.

So, as you read this, think to yourself whether you are measuring up when it comes to character. Examine your life so that it is truly worth living. And think about the qualities of character you need to live to win.

Character Strikes The Last Blow

Character enables us to do what is right for the right reasons. When we act with good character, we develop integrity and gain the inner sense of satisfaction that comes with it. When we know that we have done right, we can live with a clear conscience. We're free of any guilt or fear of getting caught.

When we are honest with other people... when we are reliable and fair and compassionate, we have no fear of being exposed as a liar or a cheat. The deeper we feel our convictions... the better our character... the greater our ability is to do what is right.

William Reed says, "It is sometimes frightening to observe the success which comes even to the outlaw with a polished technique... But I believe we must reckon with character in the end, for it is as potent a force in the world's conflict as it is in our own domestic affairs. It strikes the last blow in any battle."

Oliver Wendell Holmes wrote, "What lies behind us and what lies before us are tiny matters compared to what lies within us."

The author Anais Nin wrote, "We don't see things as they are, we see things as we are." Ann Landers wrote, "Opportunities are usually disguised by hard work, so most people don't recognize them." Our character dictates how we see the world and how we behave in the world.

Character is the backbone of a nation. It's the backbone of freedom. It's the backbone of a marriage. It's the backbone of a company. My wife says, "If you don't have character in one part of your life then you simply do not have character." That is so important to understand. It is not a "sometime" thing.

Aristotle wrote, "We are what we repeatedly do. Excellence, then, is not an act, but a habit."

Our character, basically, is a composite of our habits. That's why you either have good character in all aspects of your life or in none. Either you have good habits or bad habits. Another old adage goes like this, "Sow a thought, reap an action; sow an action, reap a habit; sow a habit, reap a character; sow a character, reap a destiny." Our character, then, is our destiny.

When you consider how character is developed, it becomes clear that every leader, regardless of economic background, is in a very real sense self-made. The more authentic and genuine a person is, the more effective he or she is as a leader. Why? Because the strength of their character makes them trustworthy and believable. People become much more willing to follow you in any pursuit — business, government, athletics, education, community service, anything — if they have reason to trust your character.

In the words of the writer Samuel Taylor Coleridge, "What comes from the heart, goes to the heart." We demonstrate our character each and every day in hundreds of ways. In the decisions we make, in the people we choose as our friends and business associates, in the way we conduct ourselves in the privacy of our own home and office.

The easiest way to measure your own character is to ask yourself two questions. This is so fundamental. First, "If someone were watching you would you do what you're doing?" And then the second question is, "If you would, is it still the right thing to do?"

Ask yourself those two questions and you will stay on the right path toward a winning life.

Most of us have read about Jesse Owens, the great American sprinter, who won four gold medals in the 1936 Olympics in Berlin. Jesse Owens, an African-American, competed under the steely stare of Adolf Hitler, who had proclaimed that he was building a "master race." Jesse Owens struck a great blow in those Olympics against Hitler's Nazi propaganda machine.

But it's interesting that Jesse Owens would likely not have won a gold medal in the long jump had it not been for the help and advice of the German long jump champion who obviously did not share Hitler's nationalistic and racist views. His name was Luz Long.

Owens was struggling even to qualify for the long jump because he placed his foot over the takeoff board and fouled on his first two attempts. One more foul and he would be disqualified. Owens said, "I was scared stiff that I would blow it on my third and last attempt to qualify."

Even though the German, Long, was competing against Owens, he showed his sportsmanship by offering to place his towel in front of the takeoff board so that Jesse could use it as a marker and make a clean jump. Owens took Long's advice and qualified easily. Later in the competition, in the finals, Owens defeated Long for the gold medal.

I have often wondered if Long was worried that Hitler or one of his henchman would see him help Jesse Owens. But regardless of any possible repercussions either on or off the track, Long knew in his heart the right thing to do, and did it. He showed his true character.

Character Is A Choice

Character is about making choices in your life that will determine your future and the future of those around you — your business partners, your employees, your family and your friends. What kind of choices will we make in the future about ourselves? Will we demonstrate the character and the integrity to make the proper choices?

We live in a free country and we have free will. We get to choose our character. In our families and in our corporations and in our communities, we are able to choose the basis on which we will work with each other. We get to choose whether we will build a foundation of trust in all of our relationships and in all of our endeavors. We get to choose. These choices are based on our character, and these choices will either create or destroy.

We get to choose whether we are the kind of people who are open to new ideas and innovations, or whether we are the kind of people who run away from change. We get to choose whether we are going to invest our trust in our employees, and demonstrate to them whether they can and should trust us as leaders. We get to lead by example, and we get to choose whether we will be setting a good example or a bad example.

Studies have shown that 89 percent of us learn visually. That means that the vast majority of people around you are, literally, watching you. They will follow in your footsteps. You might say that behavior is the highest form of expression. It also happens to be the most impressive, meaning that how you act leaves the most lasting impression on those around you.

I guarantee you, if you're cutting corners and your children or your wife or your business partners or your employees see you doing it, you are making it a lot easier for them to do the same thing. If you're cheating on your expense reports or some other area of the business... if you're not giving 100 percent effort... if you are saying one thing but actually doing another... that's the example that your people will follow. And think about how dangerous that is to the health and well-being of whatever it is you are building. Think about how it undermines the true pursuit of your goals. Think about how it cheapens your own quest for excellence and success.

It's impossible to live to win if you're cheating along the way. Remember, if someone were watching, would you do what you're doing? If you would, is it still the right thing to do?

There are many people who don't mind it when you do the wrong thing. They might even like it. Do you know why? Because it makes them feel good that you're doing the wrong thing because it makes them feel better about doing the wrong thing themselves.

Character is not how I speak to you, character is what I say about you when you're not there. Character's not your public pronouncements. Character's your private actions. It's what you do in private, in quiet, when no one sees you. It's not how you talk to your friends, it's how you talk about your friends. Character is not what you say to your clients, it's what you say about your clients when they're not around to hear you. That's character. It's so simple. It's who you are... it's who you truly are.

The educator Marva Collins says, "Character is what you know you are, not what others think you are."

There's a Japanese proverb that says, "When a tiger dies he leaves his stripes behind, and when a man dies he leaves his name behind."

Have you considered what people will remember about you when you leave your name behind?

The problem sometime in business is that we look at everything as business. We compromise our integrity trying to get ahead. The former Chairman of Coca-Cola, Roberto Goizueta, once said, "If you look at all the problems of Wall Street and all the bad publicity, it has been caused by human beings with a lot more intelligence than integrity."

Good character will never hold you back. Never. Good character will help you to get ahead.

Ralph Waldo Emerson said, "Every institution is the lengthened shadow of a single man. His character determines the character of an organization."

All of us do things wrong — we know it whether other people are around to see us or not. You see it, you know it. Character is like an honor code. As I said a moment ago, it's your name that's at stake. And my parents used to tell me, "Your name means something."

In college, I was a scholarship athlete. I played football at William & Mary. Like a lot of freshman trying to fit into a new school and a new athletic program, my first year was full of challenges and difficulties. I began to think about the possibility of transferring. I called my father and told him what I was thinking about. I'll always remember what he said because he didn't have to hesitate or think about it.

My father said, "You gave them your word right? You signed a contract, right? — A letter of intent when they promised you a scholarship?" I said, "Well, yes sir." My Dad said, "Well, you're staying at William & Mary. Otherwise, your signature doesn't mean much, does it?"

I learned an important lesson that day about character. I learned the practical application of the saying "a man is only as good as his word." It's so true. John D. Rockefeller said, in fact he made this part of his family creed, "I believe in the sacredness of a promise, that a man's word should be as his bond, that character — not wealth or power or politics — is of supreme worth."

Here is why you need strong character. In your role as a leader, regardless of whether it's in business or government or in your community or as a parent, you will find yourself in situations where skills and technique are not enough. At these times, professional qualifications are simply not enough. You will need to resort to deeper resources.

These resources go far beyond technique and the jargon of training seminars. These resources are rooted in our system of beliefs... in our values... in our character.

Our character is expressed not just in what we say, but in how we act. I'm sure you are familiar with the ancient adage, "Actions speak louder than words." This is true in every moment of every day in everything we do.

A brief fable helps illustrate what I mean about actions revealing our true character. The fable describes the actions of two of the deadly sins, Envy and Greed. They were walking down a path when they were suddenly confronted by an angel. The angel offered one of them everything he could wish for. The other one would receive twice as much.

Greed, who obviously wanted to receive the larger gift, quickly asked Envy to choose first. Envy, after a little thought, wished for one blind eye.

Let me put it in more practical terms for you. We need to keep reminding ourselves about who we are as individuals and who we want to be. We need to live out our basic ethics, the ethics necessary for the growth and well-being of our families and our livelihoods.

Good Character Is A Moral Compass

There are examples of poor character all around us; we read about them in the morning newspaper and we see them on the evening news. A lawyer is convicted of laundering money for drug dealers. Defense contractors are found guilty of cheating the taxpayer. A brokerage firm admits to checking abuses. The leader of a major nonprofit organization admits to embezzling the dollars contributed by donors.

I hope that what these stories demonstrate to us, and I hope what we are teaching our children, is that greed is not a legitimate force in our society. Certainly, we should believe in the benefits that flow from capitalism and one of the things I'm proudest of is building my business in our free market system. But the grasping desire for wealth is not enough. Giving our best effort to achieve prosperity does not mean we sacrifice our character, our good name, along the way. If we do, our friends and families may be visiting us in jail, and rightly so. We need good character as a moral compass to guide us. Remember, we can't have good character in one aspect of our life and not another. It's really an all or nothing proposition.

What some folks have done in America today is to turn ethics, or good character, into a commodity. Virtue may still be its own reward, but we lose touch with the meaning of character when we allow it to be defined by the standards of the marketplace or the political arena. The equation really couldn't be much simpler or more profound. When people, in large numbers, consistently reward bad behavior, then, inevitably, we perpetuate that sort of bad behavior.

Now the economy in the United States has been really strong in recent years. In fact, even when the American economy is not hitting on all cylinders, this nation is still the most prosperous nation on earth. However, the ups and downs of the stock market should not, must not, affect our standards of what is acceptable character and integrity.

To suggest that a vibrant economy somehow renders questions of character irrelevant, means that questions of character have been reduced to a business proposition. That's not right. We can't have one set of ethics for when things go right and another set of ethics when the economy, or our own business, is not doing well. That is surely not the message we want to give to our kids. We can't synchronize our moral values with each surge or decline in the stock market. I hope there is not a parent out there who wants his son or daughter to believe that what is not acceptable in bad times is okay when things are going well.

We can do better than that. We must.

Questions of what is right and wrong require us to measure ourselves against absolute standards of character and ethical behavior. Now I know that none of us ever completely measures up to those standards, including me. But we can't set our moral compass by a shifting North Star. We need absolutes, some fixed points that we know are true, to guide us.

I'm 40 years old. I'm afraid that my generation, our generation, has become comfortable being defined according to polls and ratings and surveys. Some of us have allowed ourselves to be defined by the Dow Jones or the NASDAQ. Some of us seem to have sunk into a moral relativism in which all issues are determined by majority vote or a public display of the lowest common denominator. That's not the way it should be.

The problems that we have with character in our society must be solved by each of us as individuals. One of the things I love the most about America's system of law and government is precisely its focus on the rights and responsibilities of individuals. I talk about this more in the chapter on Responsibility. There is in our system a profound and compelling faith in the power of one man or one woman to make a difference, and in each individual's ability to determine how great they want to become.

When it comes to character, we can't improve our own integrity or our neighbor's integrity through legislation. We can't improve our character by choosing up sides on the basis of what's popular or whose political party is in power. No, we can only improve our character by large and small acts of kindness and honesty, fairness and decency, self-discipline and morality.

The legendary former Navy SEAL commander, Richard Marcinko, had this to say about the importance of character: "In my military career, the one quality I valued the most in my men was character. I could train a skinny little runt to be a veritable Julius Caesar, if the runt had enough character."

For Marcinko, character is composed of two traits: strength and morality. By strength he means mental strength; the ability to focus your mind. By morality he means decency — a desire to do the right thing rather than just blindly following orders.

"Heroism is essentially character in action," says Marcinko. "There are times when you feel like a hero and times when you are a hero - but they are almost never at the same time. When you are actually being heroic, you are usually too busy, or too scared, to feel heroic."

The same is true in our everyday lives. It is our character that determines our actions.

One of the greatest leaders of the 20th century, Mahatma Gandhi, was a small, frail man but he was a giant when it came to character. It was his character that almost single-handedly enabled India to win its independence from the colonial rule of England.

As Gandhi rose to prominence, the British initially imprisoned him. But this move backfired because Gandhi became a martyr and his cause simply continued to grow. So they finally invited Gandhi to England to speak before the Parliament. The curious crowd that came to hear this famous rebel was surprised to see such a small, unimpressive man dressed in a simple robe.

For two hours, Gandhi spoke clearly and vividly. He explained the plight of his people and asked England to leave India. He delivered his speech without the aid of a single note.

Gandhi's remarks were deeply moving and the crowd was enthralled. Although Gandhi was addressing his enemies — these were the same people who had passed the laws that imprisoned him and oppressed his people — when he was done the entire room rose to give him a lengthy standing ovation.

Afterward, a newspaper reporter asked Gandhi's assistant a question. He asked, "I couldn't help noticing that Gandhi stood behind the podium for nearly two hours mesmerizing these elected leaders and he had no notes. The whole time he spoke he did not use a single note. How does he do that?"

The reporter expected some secret oratory technique or gimmick.

But Gandhi's assistant answered, "You don't understand. What Gandhi feels is what he says. And what he says is what he does. What Gandhi thinks... what he feels... what he says... and what he does are all the same. He does not need notes. You and I think things, which sometimes may be different than what we feel. What we say sometimes depends on who is listening. What we do sometimes depends on who may be watching. This is not so with Gandhi. He needs no notes."

This description provides an excellent model of character to emulate - to align what we think, what we feel, what we say and what we do. When you are able to do this, you may still need notes to get through a two-hour speech but your character will certainly be an inspiration to others.

Character Must Be Exercised

Andrew Carnegie, the multimillionaire industrialist, had this to say about character: "It's almost like a muscle, that you've got to exercise it every day." And listen, we all mess up every day, but you have to exercise it every day so that you feel good about who you are. Building good character is like going to the gym every day to work out. The more exercise we get, the healthier we become. The same is true of character.

Helen Keller said, "Character cannot be developed in ease and quiet, only through experience of trial and suffering can the soul be strengthened, vision cleared, ambition inspired, and success achieved." Character is the backbone to it all.

The Chinese say the same thing using different words, "Every character must be chewed to get its juice."

I recently read a story cited by John Maxwell that drives the point home. "In ancient China, the people wanted security against the barbaric hordes to the north. So they built a great wall. It was so high they believed no one could climb over it and so thick nothing could break it down. They settled back to enjoy their security. During the first 100 years of the wall's existence, China was invaded three times. Not once did the barbaric hordes break down the wall or climb over it. Each time they bribed the gatekeeper and then marched right through the gates. The Chinese were so busy relying on walls of stone, they forgot to teach integrity to their children."

That's a great allegory as we examine our own lives. We need to ask ourselves, are we simply building up a big facade that ultimately is useless... a facade that ultimately will hurt us? Or are we truly living a life from the inside out that we can be proud of?

When I think back to the earliest days of the United States of America it's amazing to me how America was founded by men and women of impeccable character. The names of America's Founding Fathers reads like a roll call of character - Washington, Jefferson, Adams, Franklin, Hancock, Madison, Monroe. None of these men were perfect. They certainly were not saints. They all had their idiosyncrasies and imperfections just like all of us. But the main ingredient in their lives and in their achievements was character.

Benjamin Franklin set a standard that was the personification of the American character. He embodied the puritan work ethic and New England character traits that helped create and build what our country has become known for - good sense, thrift, hard work, honesty, generosity, and service to others. Franklin even wrote a book, entitled Poor Richard's Almanac, that I recommend to all of my business colleagues because it is full of aphorisms and lessons about character. These sayings remind us how essential good character is in our everyday lives.

Here are a few of them: "A penny saved is a penny earned"... "Early to bed, early to rise, makes a man healthy, wealthy and wise"... "Laziness travels so slowly that poverty soon overtakes him"... "Success has ruined many a man"... "Eat to live, don't live to eat."

It's amazing how appropriate and relevant these lessons are today even though Benjamin Franklin wrote about them more than 200 years ago. These words can still guide us and teach us today because what constitutes good character at any time or in any place is immutable; it is unchanging. We all know the values and qualities that go into character. Good character is timeless. The only question is whether we are willing and able to live up to them.

When you think about American Presidents over the 200-plus years of our country, what's the first thing we normally associate with each one of them? It's their character - good and bad. Had it not been for Abraham Lincoln, one of America's greatest presidents, the United States probably would have been divided into two or even three separate nations. Lincoln helped the United States survive its darkest hour. It was the strength of his character, his principles, that kept us together as one nation.

Long after we forget about their foreign policy accomplishments or their political ideology or where they stood on a particular issue at a certain time, we immediately think of the man and what he was like. What they leave behind, their true legacy, is their good name — their character, or perceived lack of it.

Henry Clay, who is considered to be one of the three or four greatest Senators ever to serve in the United States Congress, said, "Of all the properties that belong to honorable men, not one is as highly prized as that of character."

Martin Luther King, Jr. said, "The time is always right to do what is right."

We think of George Washington, the Father of Our Country. He was such a straight-ahead kind of guy that it was said "Washington never told a lie." I mentioned Lincoln a moment ago; his nickname was Honest Abe. We think of Andrew Johnson — the only thing most people know about Andrew Johnson is that he came within one vote in the United States Senate of removal from office. One vote. Can you imagine being remembered for something like that?

Harry Truman was known as "Give 'em hell Harry" because he was fiery and blunt. John Kennedy, we think of his Administration as Camelot... he was a young, vibrant leader who was cut down before his time. But we also think about his problems with fidelity. Richard Nixon, during his Watergate problems, uttered those five words that followed him into history, "I am not a crook." Isn't it amazing, when you think about it? Harry Truman ordered the bomb to be dropped... Kennedy sent a man to the moon... Nixon opened relations with China in a way we're still building on today. But despite all of the "great" things Presidents are called upon to do, we remember their character in a visceral way. We all have gut feelings about how they were as people.

For months, the United States was transfixed by questions about the character of President William Jefferson Clinton. Now the last thing I want to be is political, and I apologize ahead of time if I sound that way. To me, the issue of character is far, far above any political issue. The character of a man or a woman far transcends their political affiliation or how they vote on a particular issue. I hope that the people we elect, starting with the job of dog catcher all the way up to President, are always willing to compromise when it comes to policy but absolutely never willing to compromise when it comes to principle. I hope they never compromise their integrity.

We should hold our elected leaders to the highest and strictest of standards. And we must also measure ourselves against those same standards.

"When a tiger dies, he leaves his stripes behind. When a man or woman dies, they leave their name behind." Character is our legacy... it is the most important gift we can give to our children and our children's children.

I was inspired by a feature story that the journalist Charles Kuralt once did about a talented high school gymnast who happened to be paralyzed from the waist down. This young athlete was really good, and it was thrilling to see how accomplished he had become. At one point during the interview he said to Charles Kuralt, "I don't come with the wheelchair. The wheelchair comes with me."

I suppose that statement also reflects the young man's courage. And, of course, overcoming his paralysis even to become a gymnast of any talent, must have taken incredible perseverance. But just think of the tremendous character within that young man to be able to say, "I don't come with the wheelchair. The wheelchair comes with me."

I know people who have succeeded temporarily with vision, courage, perseverance, responsibility. But they crashed because of a lack of character. A person can achieve success momentarily in life with everything else, but with a lack of character they will fall sooner or later. History, not to mention your family, your friends and your colleagues will remember you as someone who did not possess good character.

Character Will Prevail

A great way to study character is to study those who are successful in different fields, such as business or sports. By reading the newspaper every day, as well as magazine articles and biographies about great people who lived to win throughout history right up to today, you can learn a great deal about the character you must have to be a success and a leader.

For example, I love the story of Bill Havens, who qualified for the United States as a canoeist to compete in the Olympic Games of 1924, which were being held in Paris.

In fact, Bill Havens was the top canoeist in the world that year so he was the favorite to win the gold medal. He found out his wife was pregnant, and she was due to have her baby during the two weeks of the Olympics.

Now remember, this was 1924 — before air travel. Havens could not just get on a plane and fly back from the competition when his wife went into labor.

So he said, "I can't go." He talked to everyone around him that he loved. All of the friends said, "Go, here is your chance to win." Even his wife said, "Go."

But his character told him to stay. The United States Olympic team left without him and, as you can imagine, Bill Havens wondered if he had done the right thing, whether he had made the right choice.

Four days following the Olympics, on August 1, 1924, his son, Frank Havens, was born. As proud and as filled with joy as he was, Bill Havens went through his life still wondering whether he had done the right thing. And for three decades he questioned himself, "Did I do the right thing?" But sometimes it takes time to know if you did.

Three decades later he received the answer in the form of a telegram from the winner of the 10,000 meter canoe event at the 1952 Olympics. "Dear Dad, thanks for waiting around for me to be born in 1924. I'm coming home with the gold medal you should have won. Signed, your loving son, Frank."

It takes character to do the right thing, and sometimes you don't win till near the end. But if you have good character, you will always win.

Edwin Chapin said, "Not armies and not nations have advanced the race, but now and then throughout the ages one individual has stood up and cast their shadow over the rest of the world." You can make a difference.

And 100 years from now, when they teach the history of this country to your children's children, will they know who you are? Will they remember your name? They must remember your name. They must remember who you are. When they speak about the true character of this nation, let them speak your name.

John Adams wrote, "An enterprise can never be planned and carried out without the abilities of skilled people. And those people must have principles or they cannot have confidence enough in each other."

The important thing is to examine your life from the inside out. Set your moral compass so that it is guided by honesty, fairness, respect, decency and trustworthiness. And then do your best, your very best, to follow it.

Ann Landers said, "Keep in mind that the true measure of an individual is how he treats a person who can do him absolutely no good."

I like what the actor John Wayne once said about the importance of having good character, about knowing the difference between right and wrong. In his own typically plain spoken style, Wayne said, "There's right and there's wrong. You have got to do one or the other. You do the one, and you're living. You do the other, and you may be walking around but you're as dead as a beaver hat."

It's also imperative to understand that every time we avoid doing what is right, we increase our disposition to doing what is wrong. It is as simple and as profound as that.

A study was done among more than 500 military officers who had achieved the rank of brigadier general up through five-star general. Each of them was asked, "What role does character play in leadership?" I want to share some of their responses with you because, when it comes to leadership and character, I think our highest-ranking military officers probably know what they're talking about. Here is what several of them wrote: "Without character there is no true leadership... Character is the base on which leadership is built... Character is the number one attribute of leadership... You can have character without leadership but you cannot have leadership without character..." They also used words and phrases about character such as "the most important factor... vital... the keystone... the basis... the basic element... the major role... dominant... a must... indispensable."

It doesn't matter whether it's the military or business or government or even raising a family, it doesn't take long for the people around you to size up your character. In all of life's endeavors, people do not trust their futures to individuals with poor character. A person with a low, weak or vacillating type of character may have a brilliant mind, but their intellect won't make them leaders. It won't enable them to win, to be successful, over an extended period of time.

People inevitably rally behind a leader who demonstrates sound character through sensible actions, principled decisions, and honest behavior.

The World Is Changing

In closing, I want to share with you several facts about the world we live in, how rapidly the world is changing, and why these changes mean that good character is, and will always be, absolutely essential to whatever real success you achieve in your life.

In 1991, for the first time ever, companies spent more money on computing and communications gear than they spent on industrial, mining, farm and construction equipment combined.

There has been more information produced in the last 30 years than during the previous 5,000 years. A weekday edition of the New York Times contains more information than the average person was likely to come across in a lifetime during 17th century England. The information supply available to us now doubles every five years.

The first modern computer, which was built in 1944, took up more space than an 18-wheel tractor trailer and consumed 140,000 watts of electricity. It could execute about 5,000 basic arithmetic operations per second. Today, one of the more popular microprocessors is built on a tiny piece of silicon smaller than a dime. It weighs less than a packet of sugar and uses less than two watts of electricity. It can execute more than 54 million instructions per minute.

Consider that Americans now spend more on personal computers than on TVs. The Ford Taurus contains more computing power than the first lunar landing module. And the chips inside today's Sega video games are more powerful than the supercomputers of 1976. We are now riding the next great technology wave — the rise of powerful global networks like the Internet. Something very important is happening here. Computer networks are collapsing the physical barriers between nations, between financial markets, between people. The way these computer networks connect us will change everything. The way we access entertainment, the way we replace a lost driver's license, the way we reserve a seat on an airplane, the way we do our banking.

It's no wonder that we can't turn on the television, read a newspaper, or drive down the street without seeing www-dot-something-dot-com. The Internet is changing a lot more than just commerce. Today, there are Internet applications that bring together hard-to-place orphans with couples seeking to adopt, and applications that give children facing long hospital stays a virtual playspace where they can meet and communicate with other children in similar situations.

Today, each of us wears more computing power on our wrists than existed in the entire world before 1961. Computer power is now 8,000 times less expensive than it was 30 years ago. To put that fact into perspective, if the automotive industry had made similar progress, today we could buy a Lexus for about $2. It would travel at the speed of sound and it would go about 600 miles on a thimble of gasoline.

I'm telling you this because, clearly, the information age has replaced the industrial age. Each of us is going to be bombarded with information and stimuli. Our society is at the very beginning of profound change. Five or 10 years from now we will see that information technology has transformed nearly every institution and enterprise in the world and, by extension, every aspect of our society.

And what I believe in my heart, with every fiber of my being, is that the single most important quality you will need

151

to have to be successful in this future world is not superior knowledge or some special or specialized skill. What you will need more than anything else is character. What is in your brain, what is in your heart and soul, is still the most valuable software in the world.

Remember, "character strikes the last blow in every battle." If you don't have a strong, accurate moral compass... if you lack integrity... if you fail to respect the law... if you don't maintain good self-discipline... if you stop dealing with other people fairly, let me tell you folks, this world is going to chew you up and spit you out. The fact that the world is moving faster only makes character even more important. If you don't know who you are and where you're going, if your moral compass is not set properly, then you are just going to get lost faster in the information age, in the next century. And your children will get lost faster, too, if you fail to teach them the proper values they will need to stay on the right track.

I can assure you, that no computer, no software program, no 3-inch floppy disk will ever take the place of character. I can assure you that no computer — even one that can process 200 million brush strokes, or scan 200 million notes per second, will ever be able to paint like Monet, or compose a symphony like Beethoven, or reason like Aristotle, or write with the power and eloquence of Ernest Hemingway or Robert Frost.

You may recall a couple of years ago when IBM built a supercomputer called Deep Blue that played the world chess champion, Garry Kasparov. It was quite a contest. Kasparov is certainly the greatest living chess grand master and many experts believe he is the best ever. He estimates that he can think about two chess moves a second. Deep Blue can consider 200 million moves a second. That's astounding.

But do you remember what happened? The computer barely won the match. In fact, it was the first time in history that a computer had ever won a chess match against a grand champion. Why is that? Because while the raw processing power of a supercomputer might win a chess game, no technology will ever solve the most important challenges that each of us face in our lives. We have to do that ourselves. And we will have to do it with good, strong, dependable character.

Bernard Baruch wrote, "During my 87 years, I have witnessed a whole succession of technological revolutions. But none of them has done away with the need for character in the individual and the ability to think."

As computer technology continues to evolve, particularly in the area of finance, there is something being developed called digital signature. It is just getting started now, but in the years ahead you and I will conduct most of our financial transactions using computer networks. We will make deposits and withdrawals, we will send service agreements and contracts to business partners, we will buy and sell stocks on-line, using a computer. A lot of people are already doing this. And what they use to authenticate these transactions is something called a digital signature. It is the information age equivalent of writing your name.

So you see, even in the future as far as the mind's eye can see, your name, your signature will still mean everything. John Hancock boldly signed his name on the Declaration of Independence with a quill pen because he wanted to send a strong statement to King George. Soon, you will be using keystrokes to sign your name. And the strength of the message is the same because we attach our name to it. A tiger leaves his stripes behind when he dies, we leave our name.

As you continue to live to win, you are going to be presented with amazing opportunities. You may have the opportunity to build a successful, profitable business. You may have the opportunity to raise a family. You may have the opportunity to run for elected office or to serve in government in an appointed position. You may create a nonprofit organization. You may be a coach or a teacher or an attorney. You may decide to go into medical or scientific research. In every situation, your character will strike the last blow. In every situation, your character is what will leave the most indelible memorable impression.

St. Paul, in his second letter to the Corinthians, responded to some questions by members of the early church in Corinth. They asked him, "What are the things in life that are permanent, on which we can build priorities that are superlative?" And Paul said, "They are the things that you cannot see." This seems like a strange response until you think about it. What are the things that are permanent that we cannot see but that we use as a foundation for setting our priorities? It is character, and the qualities that make up our character — honesty, respect for law, decency, tolerance, trustworthiness, fairness, duty. It's our character.

A century ago, the French social philosopher, Alexis de Tocqueville, traveled throughout America and then wrote down what he observed. He wrote, "America is great because she is good. If America ceases to be good, America will cease to be great." Since America is a collection of individuals, de Tocqueville's statement really applies to each one of us. We live in a country that provides us with resources, the opportunities and the freedoms to make the most of our lives. And what we do, how well we do, is determined by our character - as a nation and as individuals, as fathers, mothers, businessmen and women, leaders, volunteers.

Character is what will enable you to be a leader, to rally people around you. Character will keep your feet firmly planted on the ground as this information age swirls around us. Character, what is in your heart, is what you will communicate by the way you act. Character, your good name, is what you will leave as your ultimate legacy to your children. Remember that. When you die, when you leave this earth, what you possess will belong to someone else. But what you are will be yours forever. Please remember character is built slowly, but it can be torn down with incredible swiftness

I saved Character for the end because I think good character is the most important quality you can have. I believe in you. I know you can do whatever you set your mind and your heart and your character to doing.

FINAL THOUGHTS

As you close the covers of this book to put it in your library, I want you to understand something very important. You may have read each word, you may understand the principles, however, if you do not act, then you have merely wasted your time. The challenge is to make it a part of your everyday routine and then do something great with your life. Regardless of how people respond. Regardless of the doubt that will inevitably creep into your thoughts. Move on.

While falling from the sky in a single engine airplane, with no power, from 4500 feet in the air, I once again realized that you do not have time. It is what you do today that makes the difference. Put your fingerprint on your life's work.

Never wait for the right time- make it so. Johann Sebastian Bach was imprisoned for thirty days due to an altercation.

What would you or I do if we found ourselves in prison for thirty days? My guess is, very little. During his incarceration, Bach wrote forty-six pieces of music.

Susan B. Anthony was born into a nation that did not believe in equal rights for women. In fact, she was denied a math education because the conventional wisdom was that women didn't need one. With everything against her, born at the wrong time in history, Susan B. Anthony made history. Her fight for equality helped give life to the Nineteenth Amendment, that many called the Susan B. Anthony Amendment. The Nineteenth Amendment came about 13 years after her death. Seventeen nations followed suit. One young woman changed the world forever.

When France was invaded by the Nazis in 1940, she was experiencing her worst defeat in history. Shortly thereafter a radio broadcast went out, sounding a call to action. The lone voice was that of a man who had served for 23 days in a lowly position in the defense department of France. He had fled the country with no army or staff. He had been recently given the title of General as a temporary wartime promotion. When the Germans realized who this man was that was telling his countrymen to defend themselves, that he would lead them against the Nazis, they laughed. In fact, the British and Americans cringed with embarrassment. But one passionate man — one man with courage and the willingness to assume responsibility for his country— thought differently. This lone voice over the radio was General Charles De Gaulle. Within three years he rallied a nation and chased the Germans out of his country. Millions of French men and women welcomed him as their leader. When he died, his successor told the nation, "General De Gaulle is gone, France is a widow."

Great stories of great people. What makes them great is action. Action when it seems like the timing is wrong, action against all odds, action even though people laughed. Action makes the difference. So do not wait.

At the end of the day you are alone with your thoughts. Ask yourself, "Did I do everything I could do today to make my life better for myself and those people around me?" If the answer is no, then act.

Well, now it's your turn. Dream Big, face your fears, never quit, assume responsibility for your successes, as well as your failures, and do so with integrity. Yours will be a full life. One in which those people that love you, and possibly the rest of the world will say great things about you.

Remember, your life depends on it, so... live to win!

ACKNOWLEDGMENTS

In the course of writing my second book I am, once again, reminded of the fact that this is a team effort. While I may sit in solitude, telling my computer screen the words needed to fill up the pages, I know that there are other people doing the same to enhance this book's presentation.

Knowing that, let me thank Matt Sweetanos. You are not just a business manager, you are one of my best friends, and I greatly appreciate your efforts.

Thank you to my brother, Coy. I love you and appreciate your contribution to this book. You have a tremendous talent. "Follow your bliss."

A sincere thank you to Mark McIntyre. Your ability to help capture many of my thoughts and put them on paper is a great talent. I appreciate your professionalism and friendship.

Thank you to my wife, Sandy. Your feedback has helped me stay on course. I love you with all of my heart. By the way, you are the greatest wife and mom in the world.

I would also like to thank those individuals who serve on my Board of Advisors for the American Leadership Foundation. Your service is highly esteemed. I share your belief in the importance of shaping leaders for future generations.

To those of you that have been role models and lived these principles. Mom and Dad, my in-laws, and my best friend, Tom Wille—thank you for your constant encouragement.

And finally, to those of you working to make your dreams come true. Wherever you live, whatever your language or culture, one thing is constant. The dreams of the heart speak the same language. I am proud of you for your example and for the difference you are making, not only in your life, but in the lives of the people around you.